The Big Idea

Is Masculinity Toxic?

The Big Idea

Andrew Smiler

Is Masculinity Toxic?

A primer for the 21st century

Over 200 illustrations

Thames & Hudson

General Editor:
Matthew Taylor

Contents

Introduction

A

How should we define masculinity: the qualities, behaviours and roles associated with men? Although the concept of masculinity has evolved over time, with different elements assuming more or less importance at different points and places, some characteristics have been present since pre-historic times. And what do we mean by 'toxic'? If we simply mean 'harmful', how is masculinity harmful and to whom?

Until recently, the vast majority of societies saw men and women as having clearly distinct characteristics and allotted them separate or contrasting roles, with men exercising dominance in the social group.

Most scientists considered that gender was biologically determined. Today, many people argue that masculinity and femininity are socially constructed rather than biologically based.

It is clear that humans are capable of constructing and reconstructing gender identities and gender relationships, and both ancient and contemporary societies have shown that neither male dominance nor the concept of fixed differences between men and women are necessary features of human life. On the other hand, no gene has ever lived without an environment and, as Charles Darwin (1809–82) explained in what he termed the process of natural selection, environments select genes based on their fitness. It is 'both-and', not 'either-or'. If we were going to create a societal ideal for men, or women, would it not make sense to begin with elements that already exist, such as the fact that men are bigger and stronger than women on average?

Biologically determined
The belief that an abstract idea, such as masculinity, is mostly or entirely the result of biological forces, including evolution.

Socially constructed
The belief that an abstract idea, such as masculinity, is mostly or even entirely created by a society or culture.

A A competitor runs through fire as part of the Tough Guy endurance event that takes place annually near Wolverhampton, England. Participants negotiate up to 300 obstacles, including fire, water and tunnels, and contend with freezing temperatures, during the 13-kilometre (8-mi) course, dubbed the 'Killing Fields'.
B During the Tough Guy course, thousands of competitors climb over a 12-metre (40-ft) A-frame – 'The Tiger' – only to be confronted by hanging electrified cables – 'The Sting in the Tail' – and crawl through water under barbed wire at 'Stalag Escape'. Completing the physically demanding course lends credence to participants' claims of masculine toughness.

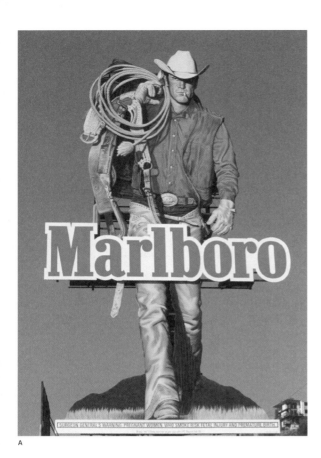

A

Ideology A belief system. We use 'gender ideology' to refer to belief systems about all genders and 'masculinity ideology' for beliefs specifically related to masculinity or men.

Traits Personality characteristics, such as introversion or extroversion, being sociable or shy.

Because masculinity is an idea, we sometimes talk about masculinity as an ideology or belief system. As with other ideas, any two individuals might endorse, adhere to or enact that idea in different ways.

We also speak of masculine traits, such as physical courage and decisiveness, which individuals may possess or embody in a variety of ways, and stereotypically masculine activities, such as sport. Masculine ideologies, traits and activities are not exclusive to men; women may also endorse and adhere to these beliefs, show these characteristics and engage in these exploits.

The thing that makes them 'masculine' is that the culture says that they are especially appropriate or desirable for men and boys.

Consider sport, for example. Traits such as athleticism and competitiveness are encouraged and built through participation. Traditionally, society has insisted that sport is mainly for boys and men, encouraging them to get involved in various ways, and fostering their athleticism and competitiveness. But there is nothing about sport that prevents girls and women from taking part, being competitive and athletic, supporting a particular team or attending live sporting events.

Instead of asking 'What does it mean to be masculine?', we might pose the question 'What does it mean to be a man?'

A   Featured in Marlboro adverts between 1954 and 1999, the Marlboro man was an iconic representation of masculinity, emphasizing toughness, independence and an outdoor lifestyle. The figure provided a clear association between masculinity and smoking cigarettes.

B   Heather Hardy (wearing white gloves) beats Sally Vincent to win the WBO featherweight title at Madison Square Garden, New York, in October 2018. Women have participated in boxing since the early 18th century but have always struggled to obtain as many sponsorships or endorsements as male boxers.

B

A

In most societies up to modern times, men were accorded the roles of hunters and warriors; they also held positions of power and exercised authority. Typically, high-status men in particular were bound by strict codes of behaviour, involving notions of honour and responsibility.

If we were to ask the landed gentry of 16th- or 17th-century Europe what it meant to be a man, the answer would likely reflect the notion of a good shepherd: someone who tends and cares for the land and his livestock, looks after his family, takes care of his servants and sets a good moral example. Collectively, these ideas are sometimes referred to as *noblesse oblige*. Wealth and power are embedded within this image, as are good manners.

A   Graduating officer
    cadets stand to attention
    ready for inspection
    by Prince Harry, Duke
    of Sussex, during the
    sovereign's parade at the
    Royal Military Academy,
    Sandhurst, England,
    in 2017.
B   Regular British soldiers
    from B Company, 2
    Mercian, leave base for a
    bad weather operation in
    Malgir, Helmand province,
    Afghanistan, in 2009.

Current descriptions of gentlemanly behaviour owe their origins to this definition of masculinity. Such a man might also be referred to as a patriarch: the male head of an extended family, who exercises control over all its members, women and younger males alike.

Military prowess, or at least a willingness to defend one's country if needed, was also expected of the nobility; they routinely served as officers and commanders. Their wealth was apparent through the ownership and care of horses and, for knights, their access to armour. Their manners and moral code, particularly with regard to helping those in need, remain with us in the term 'chivalry', from the French word *chevalier*, meaning 'knight'.

Today, relatively few people imagine masculinity in terms of the good shepherd, although many might think in terms of the military model. But which military and when? The officers exercising command over an entire battalion or the enlisted men risking their lives daily in battle?

A

Today, a man who is physically courageous with strong leadership abilities tends to dominate any social group and exert power over others – he is the alpha male. The self-made man might also achieve high social status.

'Softer' versions of masculinity exist, too, including the sensitive new age guy, metrosexual and softboy, and subcultural variations, such as the jock, rebel and nerd. Men adhering to these differing

Alpha male The dominant male in a (social) group.

Self-made man An iconic presentation of masculinity in which an individual man rises from low to high status, primarily through hard work.

Sensitive new age guy A type of masculinity that arose in the 1970s. It emphasizes emotional sensitivity, openness to new experiences and, to a lesser extent, being fashionable, while rejecting masculine directives to obtain power and use violence.

Metrosexual A type of masculinity that emphasizes good grooming, concern with one's appearance (and fashion) and being 'cultured'. Metrosexuals are presumed to be heterosexual and yet are often mistaken for being homosexual.

Softboy A presentation of masculinity that includes support for feminism and an emotional expression and awareness. It is in contrast to the 'hardness' of the currently dominant definition.

versions of masculinity are accorded varying levels of social status and authority over other men and women.

In this book, we look first at how ideas and definitions of masculinity have evolved. Chapter 1 describes the traits, behaviours and roles associated with masculinity since hunter-gatherer societies. Chapter 2 discusses the ways in which today's ideal form of masculinity can be toxic – its association with mortality, violence and systems of power. It explores why men die at a younger age than women, and reviews the systems of power that give some men an advantage over other men and all women. Chapter 3 discusses the range and variety of men's close relationships. It explores how masculine qualities might diminish men's connections with other people and reduce the benefits they receive from their relationships. Finally, Chapter 4 reviews the different models of masculinity available for adoption today and looks at possible future variants.

A Capitalism encourages competitive and combative masculinity. Traders at the New York Stock Exchange in 2009 'fight' to buy and sell stock and risk the 'life and death' of their fortunes. They wear the uniform of the business suit.

B A metrosexual coach from California, USA, teaches a young girl ballet in Nanning, Guangxi, China, in 2017. The patience, care and calmness he exhibits are qualities more generally associated with femininity rather than masculinity.

B

A

Although notions of masculinity have changed and proliferated since pre-civilization, three broad models of ideal masculinity can be identified throughout history, some dominant for long periods. More recently, a fourth contingent model has begun to emerge.

Chivalry A code of conduct associated with medieval knights, developed between 1170 and 1220.

The first model might be referred to as organic or natural masculinity, in which biological strengths dictated male and female behaviours and roles. In most pre-historic hunter-gatherer societies, the adult men concentrated on big game hunting as they were stronger and bigger, while women and pre-pubescent boys and girls did most of the gathering nearer to their kinship group and offspring. Although the roles and responsibilities were differentiated, there was no social hierarchy; these were egalitarian societies. The second model emerged during the late 17th century as part of the Enlightenment movement. In this model, masculinity also became associated with power, patriarchy and passion, with those conforming to this ideal assuming prime position in the social hierarchy. The 20th century saw the emergence of a third industrial model of masculinity. In this capitalist model, competition was added to the mix and passion was replaced by emotional stoicism. Although this remains the dominant model of masculinity today, during the past three decades it has been deconstructed and explored, resulting in the acceptance of multiple forms of masculinity and the idea that individuals can create their own contingent versions of masculinity.

The ancient Greeks and Romans subscribed to the first model of masculinity. For them, the masculine ideal embodied characteristics displayed in combat, such as valour, strength and facility with weapons. In ancient Rome and medieval Japan, a man who failed in his duty as a warrior would be expected to commit suicide rather than endure the shame of public humiliation. Glory on the battlefield allowed individual men to increase their standing in society; the honour of winning in combat was valued more highly than life itself.

A   This miniature of knights jousting before the French king and queen features in *Jean de Saintré* (*c.* 1470) by Antoine de la Sale, a fictionalized account of a chivalric knight who lived 100 years earlier.

B   The bravery and loyalty of a chivalric knight are embodied in the illustrated poem *Sir Gawain and the Green Knight* (anon, *c.* 1375–1400). In the first illustration, the Green Knight, beheaded by Gawain, reminds him to come back in a year's time to receive a return blow; in the second, Gawain kneels before King Arthur and Queen Guinevere, post-quest.

The code of chivalry that developed in medieval Europe was rooted in the idea of the elite mounted knights of Charlemagne's Frankish army. His cavalrymen were brave and disciplined and put themselves at the service of the Holy Roman Empire. Part of the code was taken from the concept of *noblesse oblige*, the belief that the privileged noble also had a moral duty towards others. The chivalric knight was therefore not only courageous, he was also bound by a strict code of behaviour, involving notions of honour and responsibility; he was noble, pious, courageous, courteous, generous, loyal and just.

B

In the 17th century, traditional notions of manliness at the higher levels of European society began to be questioned. Although renowned for his military campaigns, Louis XIV (1638–1715) of France also exhibited a keen interest in the arts, particularly ballet, and a love of expensive high fashion. The feminization of men of high social standing continued during the 18th century. It was visible in the rococo style of decoration, which celebrated frivolity and erotic pleasure, and in the cult of sensibility associated with philosopher Jean-Jacques Rousseau (1712–78), which encouraged men to express their emotions.

A reaction against these new tendencies was not slow to emerge. The French Revolution of 1789 saw a reassertion of the traditional male qualities of courage, stoicism, asceticism and public duty, embodied in the neoclassical art of the Revolution's official artist, Jacques-Louis David (1748–1825). The Napoleonic period in France, which followed the Revolution, witnessed an assertion of formal patriarchy, embodied in law through the widely influential Napoleonic Code of 1804, which specifically declared the authority of the male head of the household over his wife and children, and his responsibility for their well-being and good conduct. Power was crucial to this second broad model of masculinity.

A

Homme de qualité en habit d'epée.

Homme de qualité en habit d'esté.

Homme de Qualité.

Napoleonic Code (1804)
The first French civil code, drafted by four eminent jurists, in accessible language. It replaced the previous patchwork of feudal laws with one clear legal framework.

Doctrine of separate spheres Aristotle (384–322 BC), Karl Marx (1818–83), Friedrich Engels (1820–95) and Alexis de Tocqueville (1805–59) all contributed to the idea that men and women have separate and complementary skills and areas of activity.

B

During the 19th century, the doctrine of separate spheres played a large part in defining this masculine ideal. It argued that men and women have separate and complementary skills and areas of expertise, often biologically based.

A   Nicolas Arnoult's engravings (1687) illustrate the ideal French court fashion, including embroidered silk justacorps, lace cravats, voluminous sleeves and delicate heeled shoes. Louis XIV established a strict code of dress at court, encouraging the use of luxurious fabrics and flamboyant ornamented styles.

B   Titled 'A Man-Mid-Wife', the frontispiece of *Man-midwifery dissected; or, the obstetric family-instructor* (1793) by Samuel William Fores illustrates the separate public and private spheres inhabited by men and women.

The masculine sphere was primarily defined by (public) activities outside the family home, including agriculture and other forms of work, finance, medicine, law and politics. The feminine sphere included domestic activities related to caring for the house and the children, as well as the emotional climate of the house. Although women had primary responsibility for managing these aspects of life, men retained the power to alter or veto decisions. This ultimately gave men power over the women's realm as well as their own. In 1835, Alexis de Tocqueville documented these arrangements in the USA in some detail, commenting: 'In no country has such constant care been taken as in America to trace two clearly distinct lines of action for the two sexes and to make them keep pace one with the other, but in two pathways that are always different.'

A

The separate spheres doctrine positioned power as a male-only phenomenon, unless you happened to be a queen. Men controlled their estate's use of land, made decisions about the estate's financial activities and did not inherently need to answer to or otherwise explain themselves to the women in their lives. Primogeniture was the rule of the day, with the eldest son expected – and groomed – to take over his father's estate upon the latter's passing. Women were unable to vote, own property (except in special circumstances) or attend college.

A small number of exceptions were allowed: dowagers could own property and women were permitted to receive sufficient education to perform their 'proper' functions as hostesses, nurses or teachers, at least prior to being married.

Primogeniture The practice of inheritance of all property by the eldest son.

Culture of honour A culture in which an individual's honour or reputation must be defended against (almost) any challenge, regardless of the extent or merit of that challenge.

Good moral character was an important component of the masculine ideal during the 19th century and a central element of what is sometimes referred to as a culture of honour. A man's place in society was determined by his class and financial standing, as well as by the quality of his bearing, family, close (male) friends and any business partners. Virtue was prized, and thus challenges to the quality of his character were sufficient cause for him to defend himself (or the accused). His defence might include a public airing of the complaints or, if the insult were allowed to stand, a fistfight or duel, such as those that occurred between US political figures Alexander Hamilton (1755/57–1804) and Aaron Burr (1756–1836) in 1804 or French artists Édouard Manet (1832–83) and Louis Edmond Duranty (1833–80) in 1870. In this way, violence was ritualized and used to settle disputes. Upper-class young men were expected to be proficient in arms, both to serve their personal honour and to serve the nation in times of war.

Within this framework of separate spheres and morality-based concerns about honour, cross-gender friendships were allowed during childhood but were viewed suspiciously and generally discouraged after puberty. Among the upper and middle classes, girls and young women were chaperoned to ensure proper behaviour and to prevent any questions about their 'purity' and thus their suitability for marriage to a man of equal or higher status. Insults and other challenges to the purity of a man's daughters, sisters or wife represented a substantial challenge to his honour.

A   Needlework was considered part of a girl's education in North America in the early 19th century. These samplers demonstrate the needle-work skills of three young women; their depictions of house, garden and local flora and fauna emphasize the narrow domestic sphere in which they lived.
B   Men have often used ritualized violence to address challenges to their honour. Here, the Lesueur Brothers of Paris depict a dual between Charles Lameth and the Marquis de Castries as they attempt to settle a dispute in 1790.

CHARLES LAMETH.   MARQUIS DE CASTRIES.

B

Passions were also an important component of this second model of masculinity, particularly during the Romantic period (1800–50). Activities as diverse as animal husbandry, hunting and writing poetry were commonly pursued. Men were permitted to feel greatly and deeply about these activities, and were expected to express their hopes and pleasures, as well as their challenges and disappointments. The depth and breadth of men's passions and emotional expression are exemplified by many of the Romantic poets, including William Wordsworth (1770–1850), John Keats (1795–1821) and Lord Byron (1788–1824).

Although men's pride and joy, or disappointment and regret, could be shared fairly freely during this period, compared to men living in the early 20th century, such emotional displays were not tolerated when it came to the worlds of business or politics.

A

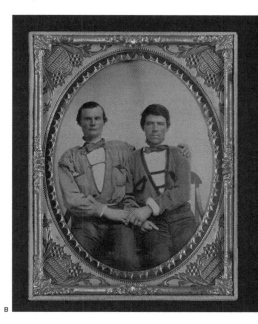

B

Passions Men's preferred or favoured activities, which they pursue wholeheartedly while openly speaking of the feelings generated by these activities.

A *The Death of Chatterton* (1856) by Henry Wallis depicts the suicide of Thomas Chatterton, a Romantic poet of melancholy temperament who poisoned himself with arsenic at the age of 17.

B During the American Civil War (1861–65), soldiers had their picture taken with male friends. In such images, they share a level of physical contact that seems unusual today.

Men's passionate displays extended to their friendships with other men. Sharing one's hopes and fears with a best male friend was common and expected, and men of this period did not hesitate to say that they loved one another. Similarly, they were conscious of and responsive to the quality of their friendships; if they thought the calibre of the relationship had diminished or if there was a disagreement with a friend, they would attempt to repair the relationship.

Most men participated daily in their children's lives during this period. They tended to work at or near where they lived, on a farm or perhaps in a local bakery, smith or mill. Once boys were over the age of 12, they would often work with or near their fathers, completing tasks under their guidance, or that of other men. Consequently, they spent a substantial amount of time with men. For upper-class men, who worked in offices or away from home, time spent with their sons was more likely to include outdoor activities, such as hunting. Consistent with the masculine norms of the day, fathers tended to emphasize good character.

Boys also spent a substantial amount of time with women, helping their mothers or other women with household tasks that might include taking care of younger siblings and preparing food. Although pre-pubescent boys (between the ages of six and 12, approximately) had the opportunity to work with their fathers and other men, this was not guaranteed on a daily basis.

Being honourable, demonstrating passions and making independent decisions while taking responsibility for others remained the ideal model of masculinity during most of the 19th century and served as the standard by which upper-class men were judged. Such men also understood that they were dependent on others for the effective functioning of their estates and business(es), and that society would judge them for their decisions and outcomes, as well as for the quality of their character and that of those close to them. It was important to them to maintain good social standing.

A

A Joseph Estabrook Raymond and his sister Anne Elizabeth Raymond are here depicted in the family parlour in Royalston, Massachusetts, in a portrait of 1838 by Robert Peckham. Both wear pantalettes under dresses, although the boy's gown is buttoned at the front. At this time, boys spent most of their time with their mothers and siblings in the home until they reached the age of about seven, when they were ritually 'breeched' (dressed in trousers and a jacket), after which fathers became more involved with raising their sons.

B For the landed gentry, father and son could enjoy roaming the estate together. Blenheim Palace in Oxfordshire, England, was built for the Duke and Duchess of Marlborough between 1705 and 1722. The park and gardens were subsequently landscaped by 'Capability' Brown in 1764. This plan shows the extent and composition of the estate in 1835.

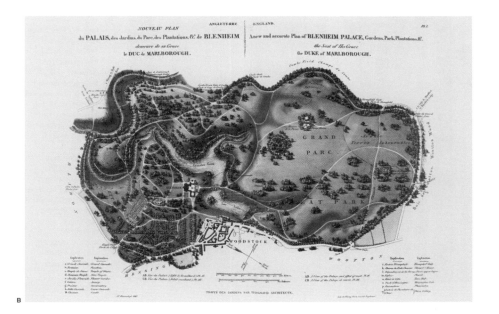

B

While living up to these measures of manhood presented challenges
to men of this class – not all of whom made the grade – these
standards were generally unobtainable for members of the lower
classes, such as peasants, frontier families and many merchants.
When the whole family lives in a two-room house (without servants),
it is difficult to have separate spheres of influence. Fathers were
necessarily involved in some childcare and child-rearing because
there was no nanny or governess to take over when mothers were
unavailable. Similarly, mothers were often involved in the family
business and household money management, especially among
farm and frontier families and small merchants.

Men were encouraged to have a gentler, more
emotional relationship with their wives and
children. The violent husband or father who
ruled his family with a rod of iron became the
object of demonization in many popular books
and plays. The influential Christian Evangelical
movement, dedicated to a moral cleansing
of society, criticized men for their lust,
violence and drunkenness in contrast to
the natural 'purity' of women, who were often
sentimentalized as victims in melodramas.
It became commonplace for men to talk of
women as 'better than us', while maintaining a
near monopoly of effective power and authority.

A

Overall, this masculinity does not seem particularly harmful for men, but it was clearly limiting for women.

Towards the end of the 19th century, a masculinity crisis occurred. Urbanization and industrialization brought thousands of people to cities. Concern was expressed, mostly by political conservatives, that men working in factories were losing the masculine virtues of their rural fore-fathers, and conscious efforts were made to encourage traditional manliness. Outward expression of emotion by men was discouraged and the stiff upper lip was adopted as a symbol of manhood.

Boys were left in the (almost) full-time care of their mothers and female teachers, particularly after mandatory education was implemented early in the 20th century. To make matters worse, working-class families lived in low-cost city housing and lacked access to nature. Many people worried about what kind of men the boys from such families would become.

Scouting was one solution: organizations such as the British Boy Scouts, the Boy Scouts of Canada and the Boy Scouts of America all date their origins to this period. Indeed, the scouts' creed reads like a 19th-century definition of masculinity: a scout is trustworthy, loyal, helpful, friendly, courteous, kind, obedient, cheerful, thrifty, brave, clean and reverent. Throughout continental Europe, compulsory military service performed a similar role. In England, public schools made it their aim to develop resilience and endurance in their all-male pupils. The schools treated the boys harshly in an effort to create a 'hardness' that was deemed necessary if they were to run an empire.

Urbanization The population shift from rural to urban residency, including the growth of towns and small cities into large cities and metropolises.

Industrialization The increase in and shift to production that relies primarily on machines and mechanization, instead of the work of individual labourers (skilled or unskilled).

B

Another response to this masculinity crisis was the demonization of homosexuality, sometimes called <mark>homophobia</mark>, and the concurrent prioritization of being – or appearing – heterosexual.

Through much of the 19th century, sexual preferences were something a person engaged in and not something that defined them. This began to change towards the end of the 19th century, marked by the introduction of words such as 'degenerate', 'pervert' and 'fairy'. Laws such as the British Labouchere Amendment (1885) were passed, making same-sex activities illegal and giving permission to the police to jail homosexual men and seize their property. As a result, Oscar Wilde spent two years in jail for 'gross indecency'. In the early 20th century, Sigmund Freud described homosexuals as gender inverted and thus gave credence to the idea that they were suffering from some type of mental disorder. The combination of changing social norms and restrictive laws led many gay men, and women, to live in fear, with few or no opportunities to experience romantic love.

Homophobia A broad term used to described prejudice towards and discrimination against gay people.

Oscar Wilde (1854–1900) Irish poet and playwright, perhaps best known for writing *The Picture of Dorian Gray* (1890).

Sigmund Freud (1856–1939) Austrian neurologist and theorist who founded psychoanalysis.

Gender inverted The idea that gay men behave like women and lesbians behave like men.

Work objects Karl Marx's term for workers who are valued only for their ability to perform a pre-defined task. They are not valued for their skill, creativity and people skills, or holistically as a human being.

A

A   Ernest Boulton and Frederick Park are seen here wearing women's clothing, as Stella and Fanny, and also in men's clothing with Lord Arthur Pelham-Clinton MP (seated), who was involved with Boulton. Boulton and Park were arrested in 1870 for wearing women's clothes in public, and were later charged with the more serious offence of sodomy.

B   Factory workers assemble engines at Leland & Faulconer Manufacturing Co, Detroit, USA, in c. 1903. Each man stands adjacent to his engine, too far from the next man for conversation, repeatedly performing the same routine task.

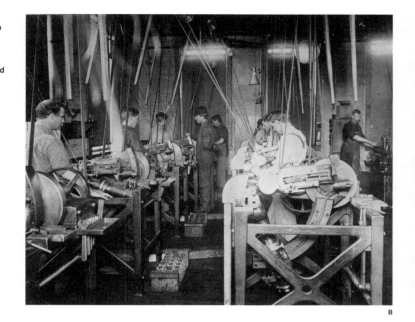

B

The shift to large-scale industrialization and mass production during the latter part of the 19th century, and the pragmatic functioning of factories using the newly developed production line and time clock, altered expectations about male emotionality. The production efficiency methodology advocated by F. W. Taylor (1856–1915) in *Principles of Scientific Management* (1911) maximized factory output but treated workers as emotionless, easily replicable factors of production. Instead of expressing their individuality through their passions or their work, men were encouraged to come together with machines and other men to form a large, smooth-running mechanism. Workers, mostly men, were increasingly seen as interchangeable cogs, who were valued solely for their ability to perform a task that helped the larger machine achieve its production goals. Karl Marx criticized this approach and used the term work objects to describe people in these positions.

A

Men's friendships also lost their passions, and emotional stoicism became part of the new definition of masculinity. For men living in cities, especially those who worked in factories, there was little opportunity to socialize with others during the day: the noise, the requirement to stay in one place and repeat the same task, and the focus on the number of objects produced prevented men from having substantive conversations with each other during working hours.

Beliefs about the inherent differences between men and women were still common and dominant and thus the insufficiency of men having their social needs met by their wives and children was obvious. Taverns, all male-social clubs and fraternal organizations fulfilled these requirements in various ways and helped men to make friends. In a marked shift from Victorian norms, male-male friendships were now based on shared activities instead of emotional intimacy. The third industrial model of masculinity, with competition for wealth and public status at its heart, had emerged.

During the first half of the 20th century, the structure of male-female relationships shifted from being 'separate' to being 'opposite'.

A The front and back of the union banner of The Federated Society of Boilermakers, Iron & Steel Shipbuilders of Australia (*c.* 1913–19). Trade unions were able to improve working conditions for their members who were exclusively male at this time.

B Tram drivers eat a meal in the works canteen in *c.* 1905 (left) and professional men drink beer in a working men's club in the evening in *c.* 1950. Canteens and working men's clubs provided men with male-only spaces to socialize outside work.

Increasingly, the man's role was defined as the breadwinner, based on his employment outside the family home. The woman's role of homemaker was centred on caring for her children, husband and house. This breadwinner-homemaker formulation contributed to a stricter definition of reason and technology as masculine, while reifying the idea that emotion and relationships were feminine realms. Taunts such as 'don't act like a sissy', which uses the slang 'sissy' for 'sister', became common in the early 20th century.

B

During the 1910s and 1920s, many women challenged men's dominance in society and the rigidity of the implementation of the doctrine of separate spheres. Suffragists protested and petitioned for women's rights. World War I simultaneously gave large numbers of men the experience of armed conflict, once regarded as the quintessential male activity, and created some of the opportunities and changes that suffragists wanted. With the absence of men, women were increasingly employed outside the home, including in factory jobs and other forms of 'men's work'; they were allowed to handle money and conduct commerce, and were given greater freedom of movement without chaperones.

Most countries granted women the right to vote in national elections between World Wars I and II. At the same time as extreme right-wing political movements, such as the Nazis in Germany and the Fascists in Italy, emphasized male hardness and aggression as supreme virtues, the cinema projected hard-bitten images of masculinity in the cowboy, detective and gangster. World War II once again created large-scale male absence in combat and female employment.

A

Suffragists Women who fought for equal rights at the beginning of the 20th century. We use the term 'suffragist' instead of 'suffragette', the term of the day, to replace the diminutive and sometimes effeminate suffix '-ette' with the neutral suffix '-ist'.

Organization man An iconic presentation of masculinity that emphasizes working for the greater good, primarily within the context of large industrial and social organizations.

A   Two women from the Silent Sentinels group picket outside the White House, Washington, DC, in 1917. Organized by the National Woman's Party, the silent protest continued until 4 June 1919, when the women's suffrage amendment was finally passed in the Senate.
B   Lobby cards for *The Home Maker* (1925), based on the novel of the same name. The film sees the traditional male and female roles reversed, to the joy of both the man and woman and the benefit of the whole family.

B

During the post-war decade, the masculine ideal gravitated towards that of captain of industry and self-made man. Men's success was defined by their job and their pay cheque, and men bought into the idea of the American Dream: anyone who worked hard could achieve success. The new variant of the industrial masculine ideal was the 'organization man', who climbed the company ladder by being well organized and reliable, fitting in with the company culture and conforming to broader cultural standards. As long as a man earned sufficient income to provide for his family, issues of character, honour and reputation could be overlooked.

Men who worked in factories faced a new obstacle: switching from being 'a cog in the machine' to being a partner and parent after the end of the working day. In some work environments, injuries were common, but employees were given little time to address their fears or concerns before returning to work. For men in these workplace environments, being emotionally present or available during the workday was difficult, if not outright impossible.

A

The nature of independent decision-making changed too, at least for the common man.

For the emerging middle classes, financial and other decisions did not have the same breadth as they had for the landed upper class. Ownership of one's own home and a wide range of possessions and other material goods served as markers of both success and independence. Having a wife who did not work outside the family home also denoted success, although only a minority of households ever reached this single-employment status. In the mid 20th century, independent decision-making was increasingly centred on which items to purchase within the burgeoning mass-market culture.

After World War II, most men gladly accepted the softened form of industrial masculinity in their role as breadwinner in a small nuclear family. However, this position left little room for bolder masculine self-assertion and many young men rejected it. They rebelled against the patriarchal authority of a wider society still run by older male authority figures and also against the constraints of domesticity – the pressure to conform, work hard and raise a family.

Novelists such as Alan Sillitoe (1928–2010) in *Saturday Night and Sunday Morning* (1958) and Ken Kesey (1935–2001) in *One Flew Over the Cuckoo's Nest* (1962) portrayed personal liberation as being achieved by men shaking off the constraining influence of both women and of a wider authoritarian society. Such men were labelled 'juvenile delinquents' and 'rebels' and became a source of popular and political concern. Epitomized on screen in *The Wild One* (1953) and *Rebel Without a Cause* (1955), their image and behaviour drew from a rougher version of masculinity that was more common among working-class men, such as that exhibited by Terry Malloy (played by Marlon Brando) in *On the Waterfront* (1954).

A   Coca-Cola advertising men in Atlanta, Georgia, drink the product they work to publicize (1954). In the 1950s, evaluation of a man's masculinity was increasingly based on the products he purchased.

B   In *The Wild One*, Marlon Brando (centre) plays Johnny Strabler, the leader of a motorcycle gang. The original outlaw biker film, the movie is famous for the exchange between Johnny and a young woman, who asks: 'What are you rebelling against, Johnny?' To which he replies: 'Whaddaya got?'

B

A

A American football, the
most physically violent
of all team sports, gained
new prominence in the
1960s and 1970s. Here, the
Detroit Lions play Minnesota
Vikings on 27 November
1969 at Tiger Stadium in
Detroit, Minnesota.
B Wounded Marine Gunnery
Sergeant Jeremiah Purdie is
led past an injured comrade
after a fierce battle for control
of Hill 48 in South Vietnam in
1966. The conflict in Vietnam
provoked enormous anti-war
sentiment in the West.

Identity crisis As defined
by Erik Erikson in the
1960s, an expected
and naturally occurring
aspect of human
development during the
teenage years, in which
the individual must
create a coherent sense
of self that includes a set
of values. The creation
of this sense of self
often involves
challenging parental
and societal values.

The focus on juvenile delinquents
marked a change in the acceptance
of male violence. Although
many men had experienced and
perpetrated violence in the context
of war, the everyday fighting and
brawling by middle-class teenage
boys was something not previously
experienced by the dominant
culture. As the definition of
masculinity shifted and the West
absorbed the idea of adolescents
experiencing an identity crisis, this
type of low-level violence became
an accepted part of masculinity.

The adoption of war metaphors in
professional sport through the latter half
of the 20th century also helped normalize
violence as part of masculinity. For example,
cricketers might occasionally 'shoulder
arms' and American football players
sometimes 'threw the long bomb'.

B

Efforts to persuade men to renounce the use of violence and minimize or eliminate their desire for power grew out of concerns about juvenile delinquents and an awareness of non-violent movements in India (Gandhi), South Africa (Mandela) and the US South (King). Concern about civilian casualties of war also rose in the wake of the mass starvation caused by the Biafran war (1967–70) and the civilian deaths that occurred during the Vietnam war (1955–75), particularly the My Lai massacre of 1968.

The identification of liberation with an unrestrained assertion of aggressive masculinity remained a feature of radicalism throughout the 1960s and 1970s. It is shocking now to find that Norman Mailer (1923–2007), a radical novelist, told an interviewer in 1963: 'It's better to commit rape than masturbate.' Young men asserting personal freedom against traditional authority and its constraining moral rules also abandoned respect for the patriarchal principles that had offered protection to young women against male predation. Male radicals were typically in favour of women liberating themselves from the restraints imposed on them by the older males of a patriarchal society, but were insensitive to the problematic issues surrounding 'free love' – as well as unwilling to do the cooking and washing up.

A Feminists questioned the definition of masculinity and men's roles in the 1970s. Here, Women Against Pornography hold a protest in Times Square, New York, in 1979.

B Male promiscuity became normalized in the 1970s. Here, *Penthouse Magazine* publisher Bob Guccione poses with his dogs and some of his models in New York in 1978.

It was this unrestrained rebellious masculinity of the counter-culture that was the main context for the feminist critique of masculinity in the 1970s – patriarchy with its traditional elements of responsibility and moral order left out.

Promiscuous sexuality An approach to sexual activity that emphasizes having multiple short-term partners without establishing ongoing romantic relationships.

Throughout the West, women gained greater access to higher education and thus professional employment, as well as workplace protection against harassment and a legal commitment to equal pay. In a direct challenge to the separate spheres doctrine, some feminists suggested that masculinity and femininity be treated as separate collections of traits that any individual might possess.

A

B

Mainstream definitions of masculinity began to include <mark>promiscuous sexuality</mark> in the 1970s, perhaps in reaction to women's gains.

For middle- and upper-class men, concerns about honour violations and maintaining one's reputation – or one's partner's reputation – had previously cast male promiscuity as a distasteful aspect of some men's character. Prior to the 1970s, promiscuous male television and movie characters were often unsavoury and untrustworthy: Rhett Butler in *Gone with the Wind* (1939) and Brad Allen in *Pillow Talk* (1959) are two iconic examples of this personality type. However, promiscuous characters such as James Bond (1961–present), Fonzie (from *Happy Days*, 1974–84), and Hawkeye Pierce (from *M*A*S*H*, 1972–83) were decent and well-intentioned, and helped usher in a more acceptable version of male promiscuity.

MEIN FREUND IST POSITIV

ICH LIEBE IHN

Tom of Finland **LIFE GUARD**

A

Masculine injunctions against homosexuality remained intact throughout
most of the 20th century and continued
to shape public policy, privileging one
group of men while harming others.
Changes to English law suggested by
the Wolfenden Report of 1957 did not
occur until 20 years later. In some
Western nations, homophobia was
reinforced and shaped public policy
as part of the AIDS crisis of the 1980s.
In the USA, sodomy laws that defined
sexual activities between two men as
illegal, but allowed similar behaviours
among heterosexual married couples,
remained in legal force until a Supreme
Court decision in *Lawrence v.Texas* in 2003.

AUF GEHT'S

EINFÜHLSAM, VERANTWORTLICH

A Four adverts
created in 1990
by Deutsche AIDS-
Hilfe eV promote
safe sex between
gay couples in the
wake of the 1980s
AIDS epidemic and
the climate of fear
that ensued. Each
overtly homo-
erotic image is
accompanied by a
safe sex message.
From left to right:
'My friend is [HIV]
positive. I love him';
'Even condoms
can save lives';
'Do you lust? Sure
but try safe sex.
OK, let's try it';
'Here we go.
Sensitive,
responsible.'

Other changes were occurring, even if political change was slow. One of the most important was the removal of homosexuality from the Diagnostic and Statistical Manual of Mental Disorders by the American Psychiatric Association in 1973. With this decision, homosexuality was no longer considered an official mental disorder in countries that followed the USA's lead, although the World Health Organization retained homosexuality as a disorder for a further 20 years. The Stonewall riots of 1969 are often identified as the beginning of the gay rights movement in the USA, and elsewhere. Violence against homosexuals, including the murder of US student Matthew Shepard in 1998 and the London bombing of the Admiral Duncan pub in 1999, helped shift public opinion in favour of gay rights, but the encouragement – or necessity – of coming out to friends and family during the AIDS era may have been the biggest factor in changing attitudes towards gay men and lesbians. After all, it is one thing to generate laws aimed at a group of 'others', but it is another thing altogether to create laws that target a family member or close friend.

Wolfenden Report In 1954 a committee was set up to consider homosexual offences and prostitution. Its concluding report recommended that homosexual behaviour between consenting adults in private should no longer be a criminal offence.

Diagnostic and Statistical Manual of Mental Disorders A medical index that lists all known and acknowledged mental/psychiatric disorders, including diagnostic criteria. It is published by the American Psychiatric Association.

Prohibitions against some behaviours and prescriptions towards others formed the basis of Deborah David and Robert Brannon's definition of the evolved industrial model of masculinity in *The Forty-Nine Percent Majority: The Male Sex Role* (1976). Sometimes referred to as the manbox, this version of masculinity consists of four key principles: No sissy stuff, Be a big wheel, Be a sturdy oak, and Damn the torpedoes, full speed ahead.

David and Brannon defined 'No sissy stuff' (or non-femininity) as the directive that men and boys should avoid engaging in any behaviours or demonstrating any traits that are closely associated with women or femininity, such as being emotional, emphasizing one's appearance or being (inter-)dependent. Because gay men have often been stereotyped as effeminate, this directive includes prohibitions against behaving in a way that might be viewed as gay. They defined 'Be a big wheel' (or status and success) as the directive that men and boys should strive for success and seek

A

A A skinhead in a camouflage jacket makes a Nazi salute in Paris in 1988. He has taken the manbox directives to seek power and use aggression to pathological levels with his adherence to the view that it is legitimate to use violence to achieve one's goals.

B In 1987 prominent businessman Donald Trump highlights what a 'big wheel' he is by utilizing his personal helicopter to travel around. He also displays all the trappings of corporate power: suit, executive desk and phone, as well as a grand view from the office window.

Manbox A colloquial term for the dominant version of masculinity that highlights the ways in which masculine dictates can 'box' someone in.

B

high(er) status, either in general or in their preferred realms. This directive prescribes competitiveness and ambition as character traits. 'Be a sturdy oak' (or independence and inexpressiveness) is defined as the directive that men and boys should be able to function independently and take care of themselves, should refrain from expressing any personal information, including feelings, hopes and fears, and should speak through their actions. Finally, they defined 'Damn the torpedoes, full speed ahead' (or adventurousness and aggressiveness) as the directive that men be aggressive and take risks. This injunction implicitly directs men to be decisive and contributes to a focus on short-term effects.

This late 20th-century industrial model of masculinity appears to be more explicitly toxic than the 19th-century patriarchal model because it specifically supports men's violence, aggression and risk-taking, each of which can cause harm. It also directs men to minimize certain aspects of human functioning, such as emotional expression and connections with others. Finally, it expressly devalues certain groups of men, including those who are risk-averse, unambitious or gay.

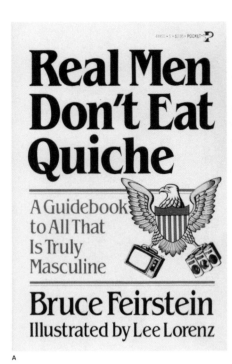

A

B

The manbox's version of industrial masculinity provides a mechanism for comparing or ranking men against each other based on how masculine they are, something the 19th-century definition did not facilitate. In essence, the more clearly a man adheres to this set of directives, the more likely he is to be seen as masculine or 'the man' or 'a real man'. Researchers who measure men's adherence to masculinity based on this definition often find that few men rate themselves as highly or even moderately living up to these principles.

But is there really only one way to be masculine? Sociologist R. W. Connell (b. 1944) maintains that multiple masculinities coexist within a single culture.

Hegemonic masculinity
The culturally dominant form of masculinity, which provides the greatest level and range of benefits to those who demonstrate high levels of adherence.

Among early theorists in the study of the social construction of masculinity, Connell proposes in *Masculinities* (1995) that a variety of forms of masculinity are available to men to enact, for example, jock, rebel, (sexual) player, softboy or nerd. She also argues that differing degrees of cultural power are associated with each definition of masculinity. The form that commands the greatest power in society is the most dominant – the hegemonic masculinity.

In the West, the manbox is the hegemonic form of masculinity today. Men who demonstrate the greatest level of adherence to this definition of masculinity receive the greatest level of societal benefits. These men typically come from the demographic majority groups: white, heterosexual, upper class. Athletes and politicians often belong to this group.

A Cover of the best-selling *Real Men Don't Eat Quiche* (1982) by Bruce Feirstein, which satirizes stereotypes of American masculinity.

B The 'real man' idea of masculinity has featured humorously in several safety and health campaigns.

C This worker at Tuchodi River Outfitters prepares for a hunt on the Gataga River on day 16 of a month-long journey through the Northern Rockies, British Columbia. He epitomizes the hegemonic manbox image of masculinity.

C

A

Men who adhere to only part of the definition demonstrate either complicit masculinity or marginalized masculinity, and receive some or few benefits, respectively. Complicit versions of masculinity are often associated with middle-class white men with professional jobs, and also with members of 'model minorities'. Successful businessmen, sexual players and bad boys enact versions of this masculinity. Marginalized masculinities are enacted by men with the least ability or willingness to meet the hegemonic definition, but who still respect the masculinity hierarchy. This includes men from tolerated minority groups and lower class men in low-level service positions. Nerds have long been the icon for this form of masculinity.

A Here, a Tokyo salaryman sits alone in a late night bar overlooking the city skyline (top), while another consults a paper at Shinjuku station, Tokyo, on his way to work via the metro. These Japanese salarymen represent one type of complicit masculinity. Risk-averse but hard working, salarymen are loyal and conformist, tending to work for the same company for decades without necessarily gaining promotion. Work takes precedence over personal relationships.

B These men challenge hegemonic norms at the Banda de Ipanema street carnival in Rio de Janeiro, Brazil. Representing a subordinated masculinity, they would be denigrated by many men conforming to hegemonic masculinity if they wore women's clothing or make-up in their daily lives.

B

Men who endorse a notably different definition of masculinity, such as gay men, are described as having a subordinated masculinity and are likely to be persecuted by those who conform to the hegemonic form of masculinity. Delineations can be made based on demographic categories, especially minority group membership.

In the Spanish-speaking world, the 20th-century masculine ideal is somewhat different to that of Britain and the USA. *Machismo* and *caballerismo* both contain elements that are also found in hegemonic white masculinity. In English-speaking cultures in the 1980s, particularly in the USA, *machismo* came to reflect negative aspects of the male role, such as anti-femininity and violence. *Caballerismo* is roughly parallel to the concept of chivalry, with a focus on proper and respectful manners, following an ethical code, humility and righting wrongs.

EVOLVING UNDERSTANDINGS OF MASCULINITY

49

Other masculine directives include *familismo*: loyalty, commitment and dedication to the family, typically manifested by supporting, protecting and providing for the family; *personalismo*: valuing the person-oriented dimensions of a relationship over the task-oriented dimensions of that relationship; *simpatía*: the prescription for pleasant, non-conflicting interactions that include social agreeableness, modesty and consideration of other people's needs and feelings; and *respeto*: demonstrating respect and deference to those of higher status, where higher status is the result of older age, professional role or being male.

Yet other definitions are available. In many Asian nations, masculinity and femininity are seen as different rather than being positioned as opposites, a direct contrast to Western directives that men are not feminine. Many Asian men would define a family caretaker as a man whose activities include cleaning the house and doing the dishes; they do not view these chores as women's work.

Researchers have also documented differences between some countries. In a pair of studies published in 2008, one Western and one Asian, more than 1,000 participants in each of 13 different countries were asked to rate various aspects of masculinity. The results are plotted on the two maps below.

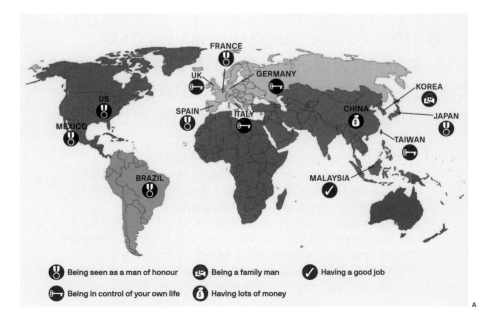

FRANCE
UK GERMANY
KOREA
US
SPAIN ITALY CHINA
JAPAN
MEXICO
TAIWAN
BRAZIL
MALAYSIA

Being seen as a man of honour   Being a family man   Having a good job

Being in control of your own life   Having lots of money

A

Different ideas of masculinity will continue to find expression as people explore the qualities, behaviours and roles associated with today's hegemonic form of masculinity. The impact of the more malign competitive and aggressive tenets of the manbox on individuals and society will continue to be highlighted and questioned by many in the search for less harmful forms of masculinity. Multiple forms of masculinity already coexist, and the idea that individuals are free to create their own contingent models of masculinity is now being discussed.

A   World map showing the most highly rated components of masculinity in each of 13 countries, according to a pair of 2008 studies. Being a man of honour and being in control of your own life were rated the most highly.

B   World map showing the least highly rated components of masculinity in each country. Success with women and being physically attractive were ranked the least important components of masculinity today.

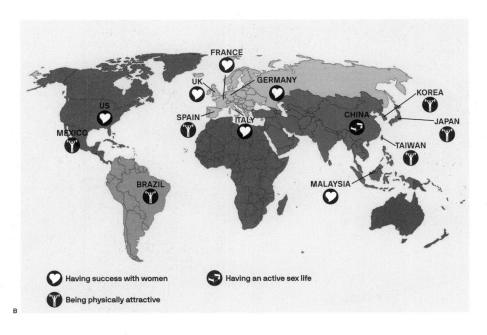

FRANCE
UK
GERMANY
KOREA
US
SPAIN
ITALY
CHINA
JAPAN
MEXICO
TAIWAN
BRAZIL
MALAYSIA

♥ Having success with women   🔄 Having an active sex life

🏋 Being physically attractive

B

A

Heterosexism A set of behaviours, values and attitudes that reflect a belief in the primacy of those whose romantic and sexual behaviours occur only in male-female pairings and not in other types of pairings (eg homosexual, bisexual).

Power has been central to the hegemonic definition of masculinity since the late 17th century, and this has facilitated sexism, racism and heterosexism. Directives to obtain status and be ambitious make this focus on power explicit, while encouragement to be decisive, take risks and act – rather than think or feel – all support the acquisition of power.

The tolerance for violence that is included in the adventurousness and aggressiveness directive provides a particularly dangerous method for achieving high status.

From a sociological perspective, male power in Western nations has been centralized in and dominated by men who are white, relatively well-educated, heterosexual and from the upper classes. In this chapter, we examine the ways in which the currently dominant Western definition of masculinity – the manbox – contributes to men's power to harm themselves, other men and women.

Globally, men die younger than women and the magnitude of this discrepancy varies from one country to the next. In Iceland, Ireland, Malta, the Netherlands, Norway, Sweden and the Republic of Macedonia, men live 'only' four years less than women, which places these countries among those with the smallest differentials. By contrast, men die approximately ten years younger than women in Belarus, Lithuania, Latvia, the Russian Federation and Ukraine.

Being born male has typically been among the first determinants of whether an individual is eligible to serve in a nation's military, in combination with age and fitness. Only in the past few decades have some nations opened military positions, including combat and front line service, to all citizens who are of age and sufficiently fit, regardless of gender.

A   Actors Sylvester Stallone, Arnold Schwarzenegger and Jean-Claude Van Damme popularized the muscled hero of action movies of the 1980s and 1990s. They helped promote the idea that violence was an acceptable and even desirable component of masculinity.

B   Two members of the violent 18th Street gang in Quezaltepeque, El Salvador, during a peace conference with the country's government in 2012.

The acceptance that violence is an integral part of enacting power is a key reason men's lives are shorter than those of women. Men kill men at notably higher rates via homicide and war; what could be a clearer indication of power than killing? In both cases, the vast majority of victims – and killers – are younger men, aged between 15 and 39. In the USA, for example, 75 to 80% of homicide victims each year are men.

A

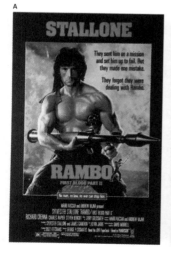

B

Men who commit assault, rape and murder typically report pathological levels of adherence to the power aspects of hegemonic masculinity and often do so in a rigid fashion that disallows or disavows other versions of masculinity and resists changes to the definition of masculinity. Their willingness to be violent may be a way to avoid being dominated by another man (as women are), also signified by sexist comments and behaviours. In addition, violence provides a method of gaining status or respect, by literally beating one's opponents and thus moving up the dominance hierarchy and potentially proving oneself to be the alpha male. Overpowering a partner to convince, or intimidate, them to have sex can also provide status because the man can then claim another sexual conquest and burnish his credential as promiscuous.

A

Violent men also tend to have difficulty with emotions such as sadness or anxiety, often displaying them as anger and identifying other people as the cause of these feelings. They then act against those individuals in order to remove the source of their anger. Like most people, violent men tend to find friends who hold similar values and perspectives. Given their adherence to the dominant definition of masculinity, they have little opportunity to address their feelings in a non-violent manner and little pressure to do so. Many violent men also report that they grew up in households or neighbour-hoods where violence was common, including abuse within the household such as spousal abuse, abuse of children or both.

Mass murders, which involve the killing of four or more individuals, have been almost exclusively perpetrated by men, and mostly in the USA. Some murderers see themselves as part of a larger 'army' that is defending their group (religion, nation, etc) against others and for which there is no other viable method of defence, as exemplified by the Tree of Life shootings in Pittsburgh, USA, in October 2018. In most scenarios, these men have few other successes and low status, and thus fit the general profile of the men who are most likely to be violent.

Tree of Life shootings
The murder of eleven Jewish worshippers at the Tree of Life Synagogue in Pittsburgh during the Sabbath on 27 October 2018.

A Members of the Grape Street Watts Crips – a Los Angeles street gang – fought a violent turf war with the Bounty Hunter Bloods during the 1980s. Most members of both gangs were African American, thus provoking discussion of black-on-black violence. Three young 'wannabe' members of the Dodge City Crips (San Pedro) pose for the camera (below right).

B People dive for cover at Route 91 Harvest country music festival in Las Vegas in 2017 after gunfire was heard. Most of the victims (58 fatalities, 422 wounded) were white, as was the shooter. The FBI found no evidence of ideological or personal motives.

Other murderers, particularly those who perpetrate family mass murders or workplace shootings, are often prompted by the loss of a romantic partner or job. Seeing themselves as having no other meaningful method to address their emotional pain, they blame their ex-partner or ex-boss and take revenge. Such shootings almost always include the death of the murderer, sometimes as 'death by cop' because the perpetrator refuses to surrender. These motives are virtually identical to those for suicide.

B

The vast majority of all murderers and violent criminals are men.

In the USA, which has the highest rates of violence in the Western world, men commit approximately 90% of murders. The murderer and his victim are usually members of the same racial group.

Incarceration rates, especially for serious crimes or felonies, often demonstrate racial disparities. Black men are particularly over-represented among those jailed in Britain and the USA, a dramatic reflection of the idea that black masculinity is subordinated.

Suicide is the ultimate self-harm and men take their own lives at higher rates than women in nearly every country around the globe. The World Health Organization reports that men are 1.8 times more likely than women to complete

SAVE THE MALE

A

B

a suicide attempt. In the USA, men are more lethal than women with every method, and they tend to choose more effective methods of suicide (firearms as opposed to a medication overdose, for example). Male lethality may be the result of hegemonic masculinity's focus on being an efficient problem solver and choosing action over (extended) reflection.

Does the manbox contribute to men's suicidality?

Masculine norms discourage men from expressing or examining their feelings in depth, and instead encourage men to 'have a stiff upper lip' and 'play through the pain'. This results in many men grappling alone with a problem they are unable to solve, which may exacerbate their sense of helplessness and failure.

A   Adverts placed in magazines in 2012 (left) and 2017 by Campaign Against Living Miserably (CALM), a movement against male suicide based in Britain.

B   Many men find it difficult to discuss depression. A campaign by CALM in 2018 drew attention to the issue of male suicide by placing 84 life-sized sculptures by Mark

Jenkins on the roof of ITV Television Centre, London. The 84 sculptures represented the number of men who take their own life every week in Britain.

A

Such feelings are characteristic of clinical depression. For decades, women have been diagnosed with this disorder at higher rates than men. Some authors have suggested that the diagnostic criteria of clinical depression disfavour men and that men's displays of depressive symptoms are more closely aligned with the psychological framework that underlies alcoholism and long-term substance abuse.

A   Many men mask their depression by drinking alcohol. Here, two men pass out after drinking heavily in County Clare, Ireland, in 1982.

B   A Lafayette Jefferson senior suffers concussion during a football game in 2010. The players' helmets were fitted with accelerometers in order to study concussions.

C   Cross sections of a normal brain (top) and the depleted brain of former University of Texas football player Greg Ploetz at stage 4 of CTE.

Self-perceived failures that are likely to increase thoughts of suicide are often related to the loss of a long-term partner or job. It may be an actual loss – separation/divorce, being fired or made redundant – or an anticipated loss – fear of the end of a long-term romantic relationship, not receiving an expected job offer or promotion. Globally, a man is most likely to take his own life between the ages of 30 and 49. Boys' and men's (non-suicidal) self-harm appears to be driven by similar motivations. Creating a positive state by focusing on the act of self-harm and drawing attention to one's self – a 'cry for help' – are also common motives, at least among adolescents and young adults. Globally, self-harm is more common among those raised in abusive households and those who report depressive symptoms, both of which can contribute to a sense of powerlessness. Drinking alcohol immediately prior to or during self-harm is also typical.

Clinical depression
A mental health diagnosis characterized by persistent or long-term feelings of depression or worthlessness. The disorder is associated with difficulty motivating oneself to complete daily tasks, such as getting out of bed, going to work and showering, and also with a loss of interest in previously enjoyable activities, such as hobbies, sport and sexual activity.

Substance abuse The overuse and misuse of substances such as alcohol, marijuana and other illicit drugs. Abuse refers to a time period prior to 'dependence', both of which may be considered 'addiction'.

Chronic traumatic encephalopathy (CTE)
A degenerative brain disease in which a protein called tau forms clumps that slowly spread throughout the brain, killing brain cells.

Degenerative dementia
The ongoing loss of mental functions, such as organization, planning and emotional regulation, due to brain degeneration or injury. Changes to personality may also occur.

The manbox dictate regarding risk-taking encourages some lifestyle choices that lead to avoidable injuries and, in some cases, death.

In the past decade, the deleterious effects of chronic traumatic encephalopathy (CTE), specifically long-term brain injuries, among retired athletes has become increasingly apparent. CTE appears to be the result of repeated head impacts, such as might occur in soccer or American football. The symptoms of CTE include impulse control problems, depression, confusion, aggression and degenerative dementia. Although the benefits of being a successful athlete include substantial financial and status rewards, many are now asking if the payoff is worth the risk, given the extremely low chances of success.

B

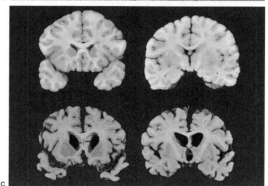
C

A

Masculine adventurousness helps explain why men and boys die from accidental causes more often than women and girls.

For every country in Europe, as well as Canada, Australia and the USA, men die twice as often as women as a result of car accidents and four times as often by drowning; they are 18 times more likely than women to die at work. Many of these deaths can be linked directly to cultural norms that encourage, and sometimes facilitate, male risk-taking. The promotion of men who are the first to explore a place, such as Antarctica, or who complete the most daring and dangerous feats in sporting competitions, including surfing and Formula 1, and our provision of additional pay to those in dangerous jobs, such as skyscraper construction, represent cultural pay-offs for male risk-taking.

B

A   Rubens Barrichello makes a pit stop during the Chinese F1 Grand Prix in 2005. While fatalities are rare among professional drivers, masculine adventurousness leads to risky driving on regular roads and a high level of fatalities among young male drivers.

B   Spanish matador El Cordobés is gored by a bull during a bullfight at La Misericordia bullring, Zaragoza, Spain, in 2013. Such a high level of physical danger is acceptable to only a very few men.

Globally, men die approximately three times more often than women from a range of mouth and lip cancers, which are primarily linked to smoking, and they die two to three times more often from alcohol use and substance abuse (together). These are preventable deaths.

Some of these cancers, and the deaths they cause, are the result of men's attempts to conform to the cultural reinforcement of hegemonic masculinity. Until the 1990s, advertisements for tobacco in the USA often suggested or explicitly stated that the products were masculine, with the Marlboro man and Joe Camel depicting male lifestyles such as the old West and urban sophistication. Beer commercials often link consumption to athleticism and success with women: at the end of each commercial from the 2006–18 campaign, Dos Equis's 'most interesting man in the world', who appeared to be in his fifties, was often pictured with two beautiful women in their twenties.

Men's desire to appear invulnerable and in control, and thus their unwillingness to acknowledge problems or seek help, contributes to their relatively poor health compared to women. Men are less likely to consult a doctor than women. When they eventually arrive at the surgery with a health concern, their condition is more likely to be severe, which often limits the treatment options and leads to shorter life expectancy.

Quite apart from the prohibitive cost of health care for some in a number of countries, men's access to health care is also influenced by their working conditions. Individuals in professional positions typically have greater flexibility in their work hours, greater opportunity to work from home and greater ability to take time off, while those in hourly positions have less flexibility and may lose income if they are absent. For men whose self-worth is largely related to their ability to function as a breadwinner, such problems serve to discourage self-care.

A

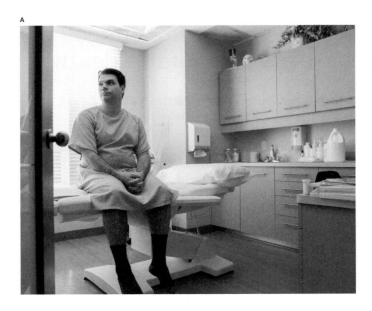

A   Being a medical patient places men in a powerless, vulnerable role, a position feared by those men who most closely identify with hegemonic masculinity.

B   Competitors at the Czech national bodybuilding championship wait their turn to be assessed.

C   Changes in our conception of the ideal male physique have contributed to greater numbers of men seeking cosmetic surgery. This man has had liposuction on his right side.

B

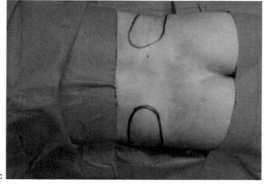

C

The desire to look physically strong and powerful can cause men to have poor or complicated relationships with their bodies. The struggle to be ever more 'cut' can interfere with some men's routine functioning and mental health. The symptomatology and psychological factors are, in fact, quite similar to those that individuals with anorexia report. Colloquially, this is sometimes referred to as 'bigorexia'; officially, these men may be suffering from body dysmorphic disorder.

Today's male models, who often visually represent the standard of male health, have better muscle definition than those working a few decades ago. This is also true for male actors, particularly those who make action movies. A comparison of James Bond actors Sean Connery (b. 1930) and Daniel Craig (b. 1968) illustrates the differences in physical fitness and muscular definition. It also makes apparent another difference: Connery has chest hair and Craig does not, and nor do most male models or male action film stars today, who routinely appear shirtless. Standards have shifted to a hairless ideal, paralleling encouragement for women to be hairless from the neck down.

A

These changes are also present in the images and products aimed at young boys. Comparisons of action figures – they are not dolls – from when the movie *Star Wars* was first released in 1977 and again when it was re-released 20 years later reveal substantial improvement in the muscle definition of Luke Skywalker and Han Solo. (Barbie isn't the only one to have plastic surgery!) Many superheroes – or rather, the actors who portray these characters on screen – have become more muscular, too.

A   These wrestling action figures for sale in a second-hand market in Fuengirola, Spain, present an idealized model of masculinity that is unachievable for most men.

B   Here, Supreme Court and High Court judges gather at Westminster Abbey, London, in 2018, ahead of the annual service to mark the start of the legal year. Laws were made by men and still tend to advantage some groups of men over others and over women.

So, some individual men make choices that harm themselves and some of these decisions are related to masculine directives, although financial pressures are influential, too. But what about the broader sociological level? Does hegemonic masculinity have toxic effects on a larger scale?

CHAPTER 2

B

Patriarchy A system of organizing cultural power that provides advantages to men who fit certain demographic categories and who most clearly enact a culture's desired form of (hegemonic) masculinity. The advantages may be provided via legal mechanisms or cultural norms that support discrimination.

Kyriarchy A term for the interlocking set of systems of power – economic, political, religious, class, gender, etc – that does not prioritize one system over another.

Men have long dominated the political, legal, economic and cultural systems that have shaped nations. They have used their power to codify and structure laws in ways that provide advantages to some groups of men at the cost of others, and that are less available or unavailable to women. What better way to ensure power for the group called men than by creating laws and customs that give men advantages that women don't have? Women are also devalued in male-oriented culture, with boys using slurs such as 'don't be such a girl'. This structure and these systems are referred to as patriarchy. A newer term, kyriarchy, refers to the interlocking systems of power without inherently implying that gender is the dominant organizing one.

A

Feminist scholars have identified a number of sexist practices that promote men's power and status while minimizing those of women. Differential pay for men and women doing the same or a similar job is one such mechanism. Placing a lower financial value on work traditionally done by women also contributes to an overall gender wage gap.

Men's use of power to control others has not been limited to the suppression of women. White men in much of Europe and the Americas exercised power over non-whites through laws and customs that prevented men in those groups from obtaining power. Limits on property ownership, poorer access to education and a range of other practices, including slavery and immigration policies, have all been used to promote one racial group over another. Heterosexual men have also assumed superiority over homosexual men through laws and cultural slurs such as 'fag'.

These practices and belief systems – sexism, racism and heterosexism – can all be seen as ways in which certain groups of men obtain and hold power over women and other groups of men. The cost to these 'others' can vary widely. At the individual level, they may impede workplace advancement and thus contribute to the wage gap, they may increase one's susceptibility to unprovoked violent attack, such as murder or rape, or they may rob an individual of their self-esteem or belief in their ability to thrive, due to persistent messages that they are 'less than'. At the group level, these practices can lead to mass incarceration, persistent poverty and (chronic) underachievement, which marks these groups as 'unwilling' to work hard while also receiving more than their fair share of public resources.

A   US President Trump signs an executive order banning federal funding of abortions overseas in the Oval Office of the White House. He is witnessed by his senior advisors, all of whom are white men.

B   The Women's Institute of Policy Research reviewed income levels in the USA in 2016 and found that a wage gap between men and women still exists. This illustration by Sarah Gochrach, taken from the documentary film *Equal Means Equal*, shows how much a white woman, an African American woman and a Latino woman earn in relation to a white man, based on median annual full-time earnings.

Sexist A term that refers to a set of behaviours, values and attitudes that reflect a belief in the innate superiority of men over women. It may occur at both individual and societal levels.

Wage gap The disparity in wages between two groups, especially for the same position or type of work. Differences are often reported based on demographic categories such as gender or ethnicity.

B

Some men assert that we should stop trying to change them because men are naturally oriented towards power, and the outcomes described here are inevitable consequences of that inclination. Some of these men have become a political movement, identifying themselves as men's rights activists (MRAs).

Their version of masculinity emphasizes men's dominance over women, disparages gay men and prizes power. They are easy to find online but do not have a meaningful presence among academics or organized activists. Online, they often threaten real-world violence and swarm individuals they object to. Their actions have caused journalist Jessica Valenti (for her writing) and actor Leslie Jones (for starring in the *Ghostbusters* remake) to leave social media platforms. As gender studies author Christa Hodapp explained in 2017, the MRA's decision to engage in online trolling is an unusual political strategy but the only available option because they cannot engage with the dominant gynocentric culture.

A

Men's rights activists (MRAs) Individuals who advocate for a version f masculinity characterized by misogyny, heterosexism and the use of violence in support of their principles.

Gynocentric culture The idea that a culture is dominated by a focus on women and women's issues.

Incels Short for 'involuntary celibates'. The term is adopted by men who have been repeatedly frustrated in their attempts to have sex with women despite their own belief that they are sufficiently attractive and doing all the right things.

B

Within the MRA universe, some men self-identify as involuntary celibates or incels. They emphasize male dominance over women and downplay notions of equality, with some arguing that women should be excluded from the workplace to ensure their financial dependence on men. These men buy into the stereotype of men as being promiscuous; they hold sexist beliefs and often believe that it is women's duty to fulfil men's sexual desires. Online, chat rooms and messages boards frequented by incels often demonstrate extreme disrespect for and degradation of women, including encouragement for men to be violent towards women who refuse men's sexual advances. US mass shooter Elliot Rodger (2014) and Canadian van attack killer Alek Minassian (2018) both posted in incel chat rooms.

A   Santa Barbara County Sheriff identifies murder suspect Elliot Rodger at a press conference in 2014 (top). Rodger stabbed three people to death at his apartment before shooting to death three more in a mass killing spree. Flowers mark the place where his victims died (bottom). Rodger had intended to kill women indiscriminately due to his persistent inability to attract romantic or sexual partners.

B   Decorating rooms with cute female anime figures is widespread in Tokyo. Some men develop romantic feelings for anime-decorated body pillows. A 'waifu' can be a substitute for a relationship with a real woman.

Julien
Now say 'Daddy can I have your phone number?' and then start barking like a dog.

A

Incels often argue that if a man has followed the traditional script for a heterosexual date – asking out a woman, making polite conversation, paying for the evening – then she is obliged to be sexual with him. In essence, these men believe that a woman's consent for a first date, combined with not leaving in the middle of the date, is a promise of, and consent for, later sexual activity.

Many MRAs are fond of pointing out that #NotAllMen engage in whatever behaviour or set of beliefs is under discussion, and subsequently refuse to participate in conversations that point to men in general. While the claim that not all men do 'X' is true, it does not invalidate any of the data reported here or elsewhere. This use of #NotAllMen makes it more difficult to address any problematic issues. In essence, most men's proper behaviour becomes a shield for some men's misbehaviour.

#NotAllMen A hashtag and style of argument in which the user refuses to allow the conversation to move forward until their adversary acknowledges that a general claim about men does not apply to all men.

Politicians such as Mike Buchanan (b. 1957), leader of Britain's Justice for Men and Boys (and the Women Who Love Them) party, and Donald Trump (b. 1946) appear to hold beliefs that are consistent with MRAs. They are focused on individual power, with little or no regard for others who do not agree with them; there appears to be no care or empathy for others, institutions or local history. This is a substantial repudiation of older masculine concepts such as *noblesse oblige* and chivalry, as well as the genteel patrician, Christian shepherd and honourable gentleman of the 19th century. The mid 20th-century organization man seems positively benign in comparison.

A   This still is taken from *The Game: The Game* video game (2018) by new media artist Angela Washko, in which players interact with a variety of pick-up artists (PUAs) with different styles. Self-styled PUAs view male–female relationships as inherently adversarial, with each person trying to get as much as possible from the other.
B   A rally to celebrate International Men's Day takes place in Kolkata, India, in 2014. The chief aim of these men is to create gender neutral law in India.

B

A

Today's dominant definition of masculinity includes directives that make interpersonal relationships difficult. The adage 'it's not personal, it's just business' – with the reminder that business was long a male-only pastime – tells us that when it comes to acquiring and using power, personal relationships and feelings have no place or importance.

Hegemonic masculinity's directive to be independent leads men to minimize their need for other people and the social support they provide, even though humans are an inherently social species.

Psychoanalysts and philosophers, from Sigmund Freud to Martin Buber (1878–1965), together with organizations including AgeUK and the World Health Organization, have identified social connections as central to good functioning. We live in groups and we all need some level of interaction with others; people who live alone for extended periods of time tend to experience mental health issues. When we are feeling depressed, anxious or scared, most of us seek out others. Sometimes it is simply about not being alone, and sometimes it is about talking to others and gaining social support. People with social support often fare better on measures of physical health and mental health.

The manbox's directive to be invulnerable causes men to minimize their need for emotional intimacy, a hallmark of interpersonal relationships and social support. Emotion drives many of our creative pursuits and provides the highs of love, joy, surprise and accomplishment.

A A fraternity house at the University of Virginia, Charlottesville. Fraternity houses provide a place for their exclusively male members to gather and find companionship.

B In 2014 family and friends of Armando Villa called for an end to fraternity hazing (initiation ceremonies) at California State University, Northridge, after Villa died while on a hike with fraternity members, reportedly from excessive hazing. In the USA, hazing is a feature of many fraternities. The practice can result in physical or psychological abuse if taken to extremes.

C Mourners gather outside the Sigma Alpha Epsilon fraternity near San Diego State University after news that a student had died at the Phi Kappa Theta fraternity in 2012.

B

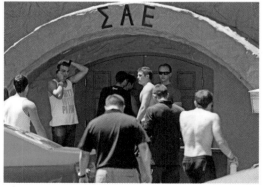
C

A

Directives to be invulnerable make it more difficult to talk about tender feelings that require a man to be vulnerable. Similarly, the emphasis on problem solving encourages men to *do* instead of to *be* or *feel*. This is epitomized in our tendency to ask men 'What are you going to do about it?' instead of 'How do you feel about it?' These directives combine to create an expectation that men will be emotionally stoic, which appears in everyday expressions such as 'real men don't cry'.

A One area in which men routinely express emotion is on the football pitch. Here, Sevilla's Argentinian midfielder Ever Banega kisses Sevilla's French forward Wissam Ben Yedder to congratulate him on scoring a goal during a UEFA Europa League match in 2018.

B This dejected German football fan is fighting back the tears after the defeat of Germany by Italy at the FIFA World Cup in 2006.

When it comes to relationships, the independence and invulnerability directives are reinforced by hegemonic masculinity's emphasis on being 'not-feminine'. Emotional expression is often seen as a central characteristic of femininity, so this directive effectively prescribes emotional stoicism. To the extent that gay men are incorrectly understood to be effeminate or woman-like, then a boy's or man's efforts towards emotional intimacy with another male may be mistaken for a sign that he is gay and thus 'not-masculine'. These directives and behaviours coexist within (younger) generations that are also more accepting of male homosexuality.

Although these masculine directives do not prevent a man from having feelings, they do specify how and when he can show his feelings, known as emotional display rules. For example, it may be easier to imagine a man 'crying into his beer' than 'crying on someone's shoulder'. Either way, he is sad enough to cry, but cultural norms indicate that one mode of expression is preferred over the other.

A Norwegian research team explored these dynamics in a study in 2012. They brought undergraduate volunteers into the lab, recorded their physiological responses to a painful stimulus (keeping one foot in an ice bath for several minutes) and asked them to numerically rate the extent of the pain out loud. Young men consistently rated the stimuli as less painful to female experimenters than they did to male experimenters, even though their physiological responses did not change.

Emotional display rules
Rules that govern the expression of emotion, including directives about how to express feelings, with whom those feelings may be shared and the contexts in which feelings may be shared. These rules may vary based on the emotion in question.

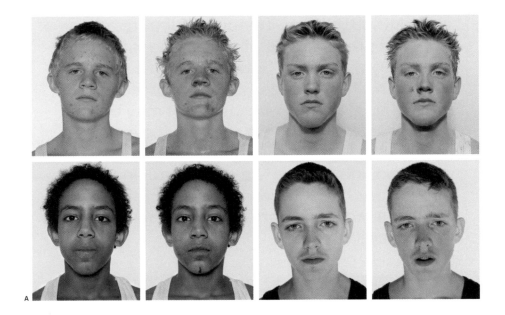

A

In Western nations, anger is the emotion that men are most clearly allowed and encouraged to express.

Commentator Don Long (1987) described men's anger as their 'emotional funnel system' because anxiety, disappointment, jealousy and a range of other negative feelings are often channelled into anger. Research reveals that men who strongly adhere to masculine norms of invulnerability, inexpressiveness and non-femininity tend to report being more lonely; they are also more conflicted about being emotionally intimate with others and have lower quality relation-ships. Many of these men claim that it is better to be angry or aggressive than to express other feelings.

A　These paired portrait photographs by Nicolai Howalt show teenage boxers before and after their first fight. In each case, the young boxer presents his calm, determined pre-game face (left) and his bruised and swollen after-fight face (right). The boxers have channelled their anger in order to be brutal, but their vulnerability is evident in their faces after the bout.

Because men in Western English-speaking cultures are taught not to express their feelings, they are implicitly encouraged not to pay attention to them. Why pay attention to something you are not going to address? And for men who neither express their feelings nor pay attention to them, there is little purpose in asking for sympathy and there may be a lot of uncertainty about how to respond when others express sympathy. Indeed, many men do not know how to reply when someone discloses their feelings. Collectively, the manbox decreases men's ability to feel empathy for themselves or others.

Among Spanish-speaking people, cultural ideals such as *personalismo* and *simpatía* explicitly promote interpersonal relationships and emotional intimacy. In many Pacific Rim nations, emotional display rules are primarily related to the desire to maintain group harmony and avoid undue attention; gender is a secondary factor.

Emotional funnel system The idea that some men funnel a broad range of 'negative' emotions, such as sadness, anxiety and jealousy, into anger.

Capitalism also facilitates acquiring power and status.

The industrial workplace and corporate culture work (mostly) together to reinforce hegemonic masculinity. The 1950s-era workplace persists in much of corporate culture today. For many employees, increases in sales and objects produced are the key to continued employment, advancement and greater financial compensation. The 'next man up' philosophy endures, thus devaluing workplace relationships; everyone understands that they are replaceable and an employee's feelings about their boss, coworkers or subordinates are viewed as irrelevant to corporate functioning or profits.

However, as Western nations have shifted from industrial production to service- and knowledge-oriented economies over the past few decades, good job performance has begun to include 'soft skills' that emphasize creating good

A

A   Night shift workers at the Hongkong and Shanghai Banking Corporation headquarters in Hong Kong have changed their sleep schedule to maintain employment. In corporate culture today, employees are expected to subjugate their needs to those of the company.
B   These Scout badges from 2014 are awarded for male competitive activities. From left to right: an Explorer Scout 'Motor Sports' badge, a Cub Scout 'Martial Arts' badge and a Beaver Scout 'Air Activities' badge. New badges have recently been introduced for skills and abilities, such as photography, gardening, camping, disability awareness and fundraising.

relationships with customers and coworkers of all genders. Today, being a good employee is more complex than simply demonstrating competence in one's job; it is about understanding and pre-empting a client's needs or wants, making a positive impression and ensuring a client is happy. As these skills are de-emphasized for boys, many men believe they are disadvantaged compared to their female coworkers; hegemonic masculinity is harming their careers.

This blend of masculine ideals and corporate culture is also present in the activities boys typically choose, or have chosen for them. Consider the structure of sport, scouting, junior military organizations and other male-typed activities. There is typically a clearly defined leader and a structured hierarchy, rank and leadership opportunities are granted to the best performers, and all group members understand that they may be replaced due to poor performance or absence. The activities are focused on *doing* – winning the game, learning a skill, completing a project, etc – and not on aspects of *being*, such as emotional intelligence or understanding relationship dynamics. Although boys and their parents may hope to develop and enhance friendships through these activities, friendship usually has no explicit value within the group even though it is understood to facilitate achievement of the group's goals. This structure is functionally identical to the industrial workplace.

A

Boys' limited emotional and relational awareness is reinforced by parents, teachers and others who help raise boys. These adults typically spend less time talking to boys about their feelings or the quality of their friendships than they do to girls, and the outcome of this difference in adult behaviour is apparent by the age of six. The result is that the average boy enters his teens with a less detailed framework for thinking about emotions and relationships than the average girl.

Gender-typed When an individual acts in ways that are consistent with their culture's dominant image of their sex. Individuals may be high or low in their gender typing or gender typicality.

These patterns are reflected and reinforced by media that are targeted specifically towards males or females and whose audiences have clear male-female differences. Boys and men are the primary audience for programmes focused on doing (sport, action movies, etc), while girls and women are the primary audience for media related to feelings and ongoing relationships (soap operas, celebrity gossip, etc). When athletes speak about trusting a teammate, they are talking about belief in getting the job done. When a soap opera character discusses trusting someone, they are usually referring to sharing personal information that could be used against them.

Fathers are often stronger proponents of their sons' masculinity than mothers.

And it starts early. Consider how you might describe a newborn child, less than 48 hours after birth. At this age, babies do little more than eat, sleep and poop. Yet, parents often refer to their children in gender-typed ways, describing their daughters as 'beautiful' and 'sweet' and their sons as 'strong' and 'active'. Fathers of sons typically demonstrate the highest levels of gender-typed descriptions. However, social scientists find few consistent, large-scale differences in parents' treatment of their sons and daughters regarding academic performance, motor skills and a range of other activities, with the exception of those that are explicitly gender-typical, such as playing football or playing with dolls. Again, fathers of sons tend to have the greatest levels of emphasis.

B

We might then ask, 'Is masculinity toxic to male-male relationships?' Probably. Most teen boys and adult men report that their friendships with other boys and men are not as close as they would like. Many men, regardless of ethnicity or sexual orientation, say they wish it were easier to be more emotionally open and closer to their male friends.

In much of the West, male friendship is often centred around having mates, buddies or acquaintances, but relatively few close friends. When guys spend time with a male friend, they are more likely to engage in an activity side by side, instead of sitting and talking face to face. Female friends tend to prefer face to face activities and interactions.

Performance masculinity
When an individual, in the presence of others, alters his behaviour to be more consistent with the manbox and appear more masculine to his audience.

A   Stag (bachelor) parties provide participants with a culturally sanctioned opportunity to ignore social conventions of behaviour. At this stag party in Barcelona, Spain, the man who is about to be married is humiliated by being made to walk down Las Ramblas boulevard wearing an inflatable giant penis.
B   Physical humiliation may also form part of a stag party. Here, on his last day as a bachelor, a man is tied to a goal post and has rugby balls kicked directly at him after a rugby match in Reading, England.
C   Groups of men are neither inherently nor always problematic. Here, firefighter trainees work together to spray down a fire in Johannesburg, South Africa.

Some type of misbehaviour or irresponsibility is not uncommon when all-male friendship groups get together. Many have witnessed the anti-social antics of a male group on a three-day stag party or football supporters on the rampage in a foreign town. Even more alarming is the racism and misogyny expressed on all-male WhatsApp groups. Typically in their twenties, these men express extremely offensive sexist and racist views online that they would never express in person, competing with each other in a kind of performance masculinity in an effort to bond with and impress the group by conforming to a stereotypical lads culture.

The harmful behaviours reflected here are not inevitable, nor do they represent the only possible outcome. Men who find themselves in stereo-typically male spaces or in all-male groups, such as military units, sports teams and some workplaces (eg first responders), often report having intense, personal bonds with other men, which they value greatly and which are a source of comfort and support.

Does masculinity also harm male-female relationships? It would appear so.

Boys and men are taught to be emotionally stoic and to not show vulnerability. If the goal of romance is to fall in love and to find emotional intimacy with a lifelong partner, what skills and experience will a man have when he enters that relationship? Finding a partner with whom he feels comfortable being emotionally open is a relatively uncommon experience for a man, which may explain why many guys seem to fall in love quickly and deeply. After all, that partner may be the only person he can really open up to.

A   An important life cycle event, marriage brings the expectation of happiness for both participants. Here, a bride and groom celebrate their marriage at a Catholic church in Kompong Luong floating village on Tonlé Sap lake, Cambodia.

B   The solemnity of marriage is evident for both couples at these Indian weddings. Many men have poorer interpersonal skills than women and may get frustrated when they cannot resolve problems with their partner.

A

B

But what does that mean for his partner? For men dating women, the woman is likely to be more knowledgeable about both feelings and relationships than the man; often, this means that she will be the 'relationship expert', who invests more time and energy in strengthening the relationship and smoothing out its rough spots. She is also susceptible to claims of being too emotional, simply because she is more emotional than her male partner and he has been taught to devalue feelings.

The man's relative lack of knowledge and skill may make it harder for him to recognize when his romantic relationship is failing and less able to deal with the problems. If he has great difficulty understanding or crediting his partner's emotional state, he may be unaware of any emotional difficulties. Moreover, the masculine orientation towards holding power may influence the dynamics: his goal might be to win the argument and assert his dominance in a situation where collaboration and showing vulnerability would be more beneficial.

A

At the extreme, he may engage in physical violence in order to retain power or control of the situation and his partner. Many male perpetrators of interpersonal violence (IPV) acknowledge this factor among their motivations. Such men are more likely than other men to be insecure and to have trouble expressing feelings such as sadness or anxiety. Many have been raised by a physically aggressive father. In relationships where men commit IPV, masculinity clearly contributes to the toxicity.

A A photograph of domestic violence victim Li Hongxia, together with the refrigerator coffin containing her body. She was murdered by her husband in Henan province, China, in 2016.

B These adverts from Britain's 'No More' campaign, to prevent domestic violence and sexual assault, highlight male victims.

Interpersonal violence (IPV) Assault against a romantic or marital partner. Previously known as 'domestic violence'.

South-South Institute A regularly occurring conference geared towards helping male survivors address 'the long shadow' of sexual abuse. It is aimed at those in the Global South.

MaleSurvivor A US-based organization that helps male survivors of sexual abuse, assault and rape. MaleSurvivor provides online discussion boards in which survivors can seek and provide support.

1in6 A US-based organization that helps male survivors of sexual abuse, assault and rape. The 1in6 name is derived from a Centers for Disease Control and Prevention estimate in 2012 that 1 in 6 boys or men will be victimized during their lifetime.

MenHealing A US-based organization for male survivors of sexual abuse, assault and rape that provides facilitator-led intensive (weekend) retreats.

Although some crude measures of IPV indicate that heterosexual men and women are equally likely to have hit each other during the past month (or another time period), more detailed measures indicate that men's violence towards women tends to be more physically damaging. National statistics reveal that around the world women die from IPV at higher rates than men.

The West's cultural notions about masculinity harm male victims of IPV and sexual assault. Victims of all genders typically feel shame at having been assaulted, but it is often worse for male victims because of masculinity's focus on invulnerability and its encouragement to be violent. The idea of a male victim is not part of cultural consciousness. As a result, many male victims report having been refused services because agencies only serve female victims, or having been accused of being a perpetrator who is looking for a victim (either a prior victim or other women to victimize). Events such as the South-South Institute conference and organizations such as MaleSurvivor, 1in6 and MenHealing all attempt to fill this gap. One could argue that the lack of support services is the result of rape culture, which tends to see men as perpetrators and women as victims, as well as the tendency of men not to address their health.

B

A

The manbox encourages men to sexually objectify their partners, minimizing that person's humanity.

When combined with men's lack of attention to their own feelings and their ability to prioritize outcomes over relationships, promiscuous sexuality is an obvious result. After all, if a man's only feeling towards his partner is lust, and he has no interest in creating an intimate emotional relationship, then it is easier to view his partner as a sexual object whose primary purpose is to provide him with a good time. One night stands or sexual hookups are not inherently problematic as long as both partners are open and honest about their wants, but if a man is lying to his partner in order to have sex, then that is disrespectful.

When men add competitiveness to the sexual realm, wanting to see who can pair up the fastest or find the most attractive partner, for example, masculinity becomes more toxic. Competitiveness can easily include dishonesty to one or more sexual partners. And if tales of sexual exploits are then used to facilitate male bonding – because in many ways telling sexual stories is no different to sharing exploits from the playing field, sales floor or other shared activity – then the deceived partner may remain an active but unwitting participant in the man's social life.

Despite the dictates of the manbox, most men do not adhere to the sexual player image, nor do they desire the one night stand sexuality. A global study published in 2003 asked undergraduates how many sexual partners they would like in the next 30 days. The vast majority of young men reported that they wanted either zero or one; only about one in four men said they would like multiple sexual partners (compared to approximately one in 20 women). And even fewer actually have that many partners. Numerous studies suggest that no more than 10% of young men have three or more partners in any given year, and less than 5% have three or more partners per year for three consecutive years. The diaries of Italian noble Giacomo Casanova (1725–98), an iconic seducer of women, indicate that he had about three partners per year.

A Male patrons spend time with female workers in a strip bar in the Patpong entertainment district of Bangkok, Thailand.
B Revellers comically mimic having sex in the middle of the street in Cardiff, Wales.
C Alcohol abuse plays a large part in increased promiscuity. Here, young people lose their inhibitions playing drinking games in a bar.

A   This gold sculpture by Plastic Jesus and Joshua Monroe depicts Harvey Weinstein sitting on his infamous casting couch holding an Oscar statue.

B   Student Emma Sulkowicz carries a mattress in protest against Columbia University's lack of action after she reported being raped during her sophomore year. She also took the mattress to her graduation ceremony in 2015.

Rape culture is an extreme manifestation of hegemonic masculinity's directives regarding sexuality, power over women and emotional inexpressiveness. Here, women are prized primarily, and sometimes solely, for dressing and acting in a sexually suggestive manner, and for men's ability to be sexual with them. A woman's value is based solely on this, and thus ignores her abilities, interests, feelings and all other aspects of her personhood and humanity.

As the term 'rape culture' suggests, the woman's willingness or consent is largely irrelevant. The allegations against Harvey Weinstein (b. 1952) that first surfaced in October 2017 and the entire notion of a 'casting couch', the behaviour of some members of Oxfam GB in Haiti after the 2010 earthquake, and the Tailhook scandal among the US Navy and Marines in 1991 are all examples of rape culture. More broadly, many collegiate fraternities and men's athletic teams have reputations for actively creating spaces that facilitate and cover up the sexual misconduct of their members, as described in the documentary *The Hunting Ground* (2015).

B

Masculine directives to be promiscuous, to compete (for most partners) and to devalue sex based on feelings of love all encourage men to have ever more sexual partners. Injunctions to be aggressive or violent, especially when combined with the idea that men and women are fundamentally different and that sexual relationships are inherently adversarial, in that each person is trying to 'get' as much as possible from their partner, facilitate beliefs that it is acceptable for men to lie, to impair a partner's judgment through drink or other drugs or to physically overpower them in order to have sex. Only a minority of men endorse this set of beliefs, but encouragement to stand with other men against women (to choose 'bros before hos' – note that the phrase positions women as sexual objects) often leads men to not intervene. This suite of beliefs, which are held by many men at low to moderate levels, has encouraged some women to say that all men support rape culture.

Rape culture A set of cultural or societal practices that support the sexual objectification and rape of women and girls.

Bystander intervention When a bystander or witness to an event chooses to act to disrupt the event instead of allowing it to continue.

Lack of knowledge about how to intervene, including not knowing how to challenge relevant aspects of the manbox, also contributes to (some) men's inaction. Accordingly, some rape prevention programmes encourage bystander intervention.

A

Pornography repeats and reinforces many aspects of hegemonic masculinity's attitudes to sex.

Primarily viewed by men, pornography, like most screen products, tends to repeat a small number of themes with infinite variations. Common themes across almost all genres include notions that sexual intercourse without a prior relationship or emotional connection is always pleasurable, verbal consent is rare or unnecessary, people who are penetrated (almost) always enjoy sex even when they have said no or are being restrained against their will, and everyone is always ready for sex. The combination of sexual arousal with violence is common, as is the explicit degradation of women.

These on-screen themes mirror manbox directives to be powerful and unemotional, as well as to use violence when needed. The repeated viewing of a small set of themes helps increase the likelihood that the viewer will come to believe they are true and will act accordingly. At a broader level, these beliefs contribute to rape culture.

Beyond reinforcing and shaping men's beliefs about relationships and sexuality, pornography consumption can adversely impact young men. On average, those who watch relatively more pornography are more dissatisfied with their romantic relationships. It may also lead young men to be more dissatisfied with their musculature or penis size, although research results in this field are mixed.

Masculinity's focus on completing tasks – getting the job done – contributes to an emphasis on penetrative sex (inserting the penis in the vagina or anus) that is mirrored in men's references to their 'tool' or 'drilling their partner'. Consequently, when men are unable to achieve or maintain an erection – or worry about their inability to do so – the impact on their self-esteem can be great.

From a medical perspective, erectile dysfunction is characterized by 'regular and persistent difficulty getting hard' and typically occurs among men who have circulatory problems, are obese or are relatively older. Men who have difficulty getting hard due to anxiety, use of mood altering substances or other situational factors, such as the first time with a new partner, rarely meet the medical definition of erectile dysfunction. Yet the marketing of drugs such as Viagra and Cialis tends to focus on relatively younger men, and the medical community has increasingly concentrated on facilitating the quality of men's sexual lives rather than helping them acknowledge and cope with anxiety or natural decline.

A   The Eroticon porn convention in Poland in 2004 featured many adult entertainment companies, strippers, erotic dancers and live sex shows. The majority of paying customers each year are men.

B   A Cambridge University study in 2014 discovered that the activation levels of the brain's reward centre while viewing Internet porn were far higher in compulsive Internet pornography users than in healthy volunteers.

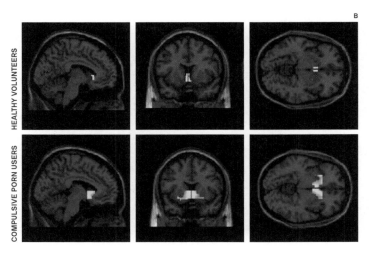

HEALTHY VOLUNTEERS

COMPULSIVE PORN USERS

Masculinity can also adversely affect men's relationships with their children. Indeed, there is a 'new' generation of fathers, born after approximately 1980, who explicitly talk about being an active presence for their children in ways their own fathers never were.

Perhaps the most striking change is their desire to be involved in their children's emotional lives, rather than to simply attend sporting, artistic and educational events. The shift away from female-only baby showers reflects this change.

A

A This baby change bag from Lillian Rose is marketed at fathers. The construction belt style with easy access pockets for 'tools' is designed to appeal to the male DIY enthusiast.
B Skoda's 'mega man-pram' is also styled to appeal to fathers. It has hydraulic suspension, 50-centimetre (20-in) alloy wheels, all-terrain tyres, rear-view mirrors, a high-beam headlight and high-spec brakes.

B

Many men report that they lack – or feel that they lack – the knowledge, skills and experience necessary to be more deeply emotionally connected to their child, even though they want to be more involved. The media remains fond of creating lovable male characters that are incompetent fathers, as is evident in the popular but poor male role models of Homer Simpson (*The Simpsons*), Ray Barone (*Everybody Loves Raymond*) and Frank Gallagher (*Shameless*). Good fictional role models are hard to find.

Even among this new generation, not every man wants to be more emotionally involved or has the skills to do so. Experience helps: men whose childhoods included a highly involved father or positive experiences providing child care for younger siblings (or others) tend to provide more emotionally attentive parenting.

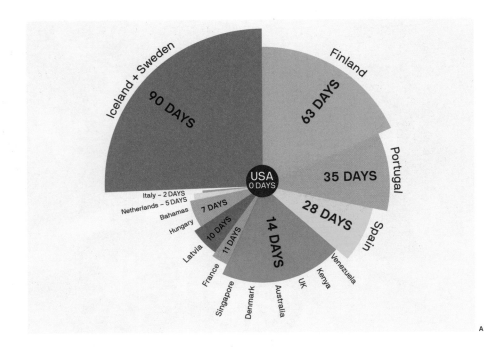

Image caption: A

Cultural expectations about fatherhood adversely influence men's experiences. Maternity leave is standard practice throughout the Western world, and paternity leave is increasingly common. At the end of 2017, almost all Western nations, except the USA, offered paternity leave. Japan and South Korea are among the most generous, each offering 52 weeks of paid paternity leave. Germany and Norway offer couples the option of sharing maternity and paternity leave between them. In Germany, 28 months' leave can be shared between both parents, and in Norway 59 weeks can be divided between them. Iceland and Sweden both offer three months' paid paternity leave.

Although we have described a number of ways in which adherence to the hegemonic form of masculinity can limit men's interpersonal and relational worlds, men often tell researchers that they are doing all right. Most men say they have developed and maintained strong friendships during their lives, and that they have made something of a trade-off between work and personal relationships that served them (reasonably) well during their working years. It appears therefore that most men today have not adhered strictly to all the tenets of the manbox, but have instead adopted a version of masculinity that is not toxic to themselves. They have perhaps created their own personal model of masculinity from a range of qualities and behaviours to best suit their personality, attitudes and circumstances.

B

A A graphic showing the number of days of paternity leave guaranteed by law in 17 countries around the world, varying from zero days to 90.

B There is a huge disparity between statutory paternity leave in countries around the world. In the Netherlands, where this couple live, statutory paternity leave amounts to only five days.

C The involvement of fathers in their children's lives, as well as the number of men who take paternity leave or serve as stay-at-home-dads, is increasing. This father in South Korea has elected to take a year's paternity leave, during which he is guaranteed 80% of his full wages.

C

4. The Changing Face of Masculinity Today

A

We know that masculinity is determined by cultures, and that cultures change. Over the past few decades, we have seen substantial changes in Western cultures' attitudes towards smoking cigarettes, driving under the influence of alcohol and the use of technology as part of daily life. We have also seen the rise and fall of some types of masculinities, such as the sensitive new age guys of the 1970s and the metrosexuals of the 2000s. Nerds have seen their status improve due to our increased reliance on mobile devices and computers. Geeks such as Steve Jobs (1955–2011), Mark Zuckerberg (b. 1984) and Elon Musk (b. 1971) have all become household names, and rich.

Demographic researchers have documented general trends towards men's greater acceptance of different sexes, races and sexual orientations over the past few decades. These beliefs are challenging and changing the manbox. New forms of masculinity are taking shape.

B

The feminist movement has explicitly challenged the separate spheres doctrine, which underpins the anti-femininity directive.

A   Facebook CEO
Mark Zuckerberg
makes a formal
announcement
at an event in San
Jose, California,
in 2018, wearing
an informal long-
sleeved T-shirt
and jeans rather
than the expected
suit and tie.

B   A male protester
at the 2018 Women's
March in New
York indicates his
support for Hillary
Clinton and the
rights of women
around the world.
Men have become
increasingly visible
in their support
of women and
women's rights.

Sixty years ago, only an exceptional woman might have a professional career and male subordinates or be a national leader (political, industrial, economic, etc); today, these ideas are common enough to be typical. Previously, it was highly unusual for a man to have a female supervisor and such a situation was expected to be a source of discomfort. Today, none of these situations are surprising, unusual or uncomfortable for the average guy. Even *Doctor Who* fans have accepted that the Doctor can be a woman.

A

Male-female friendships have also become common. Viewed as a near impossibility or exceptional a few decades ago, they may be considered normal today: most teens and adults have a friendship with the opposite sex. This would seem to be advantageous for men, as most men report greater comfort disclosing emotional and relational concerns to women than to other men. It would also appear to be beneficial in reducing sexism, because greater familiarity with members of a group tends to increase empathy and reduce antipathy towards that group.

Over the past few decades, Western culture has become more accepting of homosexuality. Gay performers and athletes have become increasingly comfortable publicly disclosing their sexual orientation. Gay characters have also become more commonplace in television programmes and movies. Social and political movements have sought to legalize marriage for gay couples and provide other legal protections. By the middle of 2018, same sex marriage was legal in 27 countries, including most of Europe, most of the Americas and nearly all of the English-speaking world. The Netherlands was the first to pass legislation, in 2000.

Acceptance has been driven partly by economics. Some companies actively court this demographic, which, for example, may account for as much as 5% of the more `than $1 trillion US tourism industry.

As these changes have occurred, the anti-homo-sexuality components of masculinity have shifted. For many heterosexual men, having a gay male coworker, teammate or friend is no longer a source of concern, although gay-based insults, such as 'fag', remain quite common.

A   Homosexuality is accepted by many
    Christians. Here, Kenneth Ingram,
    a gay pastor at St Paul's United
    Church of Christ in Laramie,
    Wyoming, is seen in his office.

B   Two of the first gay male couples
    to receive wedding permits
    in the USA are photographed in
    Provincetown, Massachusetts,
    in 2004.

A

A   Young people at a cuddle party in New York in 2004 seek physical closeness without sexual intimacy.
B   Suffering from PTSD, Iraq War veteran Brad Hammond is taking a six-month course, paid for by the US Department of Veterans Affairs, to improve his memory and cognitive skills.
C   Specialist James Worster (left) and Sergeant Brandon Benjamin take a cigarette break during a lull in the casualties coming into the Baghdad Emergency Room in 2006. Two months later, Worster died of an overdose of propofol, a sedative he had been pocketing while treating patients.

The 2010s have also brought several reports of greater levels of male-male sexual contact among younger men who identify as heterosexual. In some ways, young men's greater willingness to explore their sexuality may represent little more than men's desire to take risks and try new things.

Changes in younger men's understanding and experience of friendship and sexuality are influencing their experience of physical intimacy. Cuddling parties, which provide high amounts of physical contact between people of all genders while explicitly ruling out any potential for sexual activity, are becoming popular.

In recent years, equality movements have facilitated attention to groups of men that are harmed by masculinity's hierarchy. These men are no longer able to 'compete' for status within masculinity's framework. Some, such as veterans and male victims of sexual abuse, assault and rape, suffer from post-traumatic stress disorder (PTSD). Others, who participated in sport, suffer from chronic traumatic encephalopathy, and still others have simply become too old to effectively compete for status with other men.

PTSD is more common among combat veterans than the general population and contributes to elevated rates of suicide among veterans in countries such as Canada, Australia and the USA. Efforts to help veterans have begun to demonstrate awareness of masculinity, shaping programmes in ways that minimize or eliminate the need to violate masculine norms during treatment.

B

Post-traumatic stress disorder (PTSD) A mental health disorder characterized by feelings of depression and anxiety, difficulty falling or staying asleep, unwanted and intrusive memories (typically of harm to self or others), flashbacks and hyper-vigilance.

C

Beliefs about masculinity continue to put military service members – the vast majority of whom are male – at risk. Being in a war zone, in person or virtually, requires the emotional inexpressiveness dictated by the manbox in order to continue doing one's job as a soldier – wounding or killing others, and seeing friends maimed or killed – despite the risk of injury and death. Soldiers used to have weeks and months of transit to prepare to enter combat and to return home, which gave them substantial time to adjust emotionally. This ended with the advent of the large-scale air transport of troops in the 1960s. Today, a soldier might exit the combat zone and then teleconference home an hour later, or might participate in a combat zone virtually (as a drone operator) only to drive home at the end of a shift like any other worker.

Asking soldiers to switch from being emotionally closed for combat and emotionally open for civilian life on a daily basis is a tall order.

A   The 'know thy nuts' guide from the Movember Foundation is designed to teach men how – and how often – to check for testicular cancer.

B   Former priest James Faluszczak testifies before a grand jury in Pennsylvania that he was molested by a priest as a teenager. The jury's investigation of clergy sexual abuse identified more than 1,000 child victims, including Faluszczak, in 2018.

B

There has also been increased awareness of the effects of sexual abuse, assault and rape on male victims, largely due to scandals related to the Catholic Church, boarding schools and (junior) sports ranks. These victims may also suffer from PTSD, or demonstrate some of its symptoms, and often have difficulty developing and maintaining interpersonal relationships due to issues of trust. The number of male victims is more than half the number of female victims. For example, the US Centers for Disease Control and Prevention estimates that one in six males will be sexually assaulted, abused or raped in his lifetime, in comparison to one in four females.

Movember Foundation
An Australian organization that promotes men's health in 20 countries around the world. It attempts to raise awareness and funds some intervention efforts.

The Movember Foundation may be the most recognized organization devoted to men's health. Initially focused on raising men's awareness of and knowledge about prostate and testicular cancers, its mission has slowly expanded to include other aspects of male health, such as depression and suicide. Founded in Australia, it now operates in 20 countries around the world.

A

There have been a number of efforts to improve men's mental and physical health by reaching out in ways that specifically target men.

In Australia, Britain and other English-speaking countries, one response has been to use Men's Sheds as a way to reach out to men 'on their turf' through educational efforts and signposting. The Men's Sheds movement, which started in Australia in the mid 1990s, provides a place for men to meet and spend time with other men in a male-oriented space. The majority of 'shedders' are older men and they are often retired. They value the companionship, social support and friendships they are able to find and develop through these meeting places. Many say that participation helps them feel happier, improves their confidence, increases their social support and provides some purpose during retirement.

Through the middle of the 20th century, fraternal lodges and opportunities to volunteer in local communities often provided men with the chance to develop and maintain social relationships throughout adulthood, but many of these organizations and structures no longer exist. Sheds offer a venue for physical and social health organizations to reach men, through informational meetings, provision of basic services and signposting.

Men's Sheds may be particularly effective in response to the Western focus on youth. For men who are able to maintain high status, often due to professional prestige or financial status, losses related to age may be relatively small. But for men who are more reliant on physical skills, age-related declines are more evident.

Men's Sheds A setting that caters to 'traditionally' male interests such as woodcraft, engineering and the like. Men's Sheds are also used for male-only group events, designed to provide 'deeper' male friendships, health care check-ups and education, as well as 'time off' from aspiring to masculine norms.

A   Members of the Men's Shed work group in Geraldton, Western Australia, pose with their hand tools. Although the groups are open to all ages, most 'shedders' are 50 years of age or older.

B   Shedders handcrafting: one man carves letters into a marble plaque and another cuts wood.

B

A

As Western cultures have moved towards equality in the 21st century, discussions about the role of the father have become more common. Although single fathers account for only approximately 1% of families in the Western world, the number is increasing.

Two-parent, two-earner households face a series of choices about the extent and ways in which they share child-rearing and household management. In most cultures, child-rearing has long been viewed as women's work. However, since the development of infant formula approximately 100 years ago, and the advent of modern birth control approximately 60 years ago (which better allows couples – or women, individually – to control the number and timing of their children), the range of options for childcare has increased substantially. Yet laws and customs have not changed in tandem.

A recent report by Promundo on behalf of MenCare: A Global Fatherhood Campaign, titled *State of the World's Fathers* (2017), acknowledges that there is no country in the world where men's care-giving – a form of unpaid work – equals that of women. It identifies four sets of changes that would facilitate equality. First, encouraging all individuals to see the potential for themselves to be both care givers and financial providers. Doing so requires changing social norms, including around child-rearing practices that encourage girls and discourage boys from being care givers, changing workplace norms that bias couples' decisions in favour of female care givers, and changing national laws and policies that position child-rearing as women's work. Second, providing equality in paid leave (from work). It argues: 'Leave should be guaranteed for all care givers, of all genders, in equal duration, adequately paid and non-transferable.' Third, eliminating extreme economic hardship and ensuring access to quality childcare. And fourth, providing effective parent training that includes men and that explicitly addresses gender norms.

Researchers have consistently observed that the 'how' of child-rearing is more important than the 'who', and that men are as capable of being good parents as women, when motivated to do so.

The **Promundo** Global Consortium, with strategic members in the USA, Brazil, Portugal and the Democratic Republic of the Congo, promotes gender equality and prevents violence by engaging men and boys in partnership with women and girls.

A   Promundo staff and volunteers discuss gender roles and parenting. Their aim is to encourage dialogue between men and women, girls and boys, in order to prevent violence and to forge stronger partnerships to advance gender equality.

B   Single father Ralph Case prepares dinner with his sons at his home in North Canton, Ohio, in 2016. Despite suffering from arthritis that requires regular treatment, he runs his own business alongside raising his two sons.

C   Demonstration in support of the MEP Green Party's bid for fathers to obtain two weeks' fully paid paternity leave in 2010.

The number of stay-at-home-dads has increased over the past few decades as women have been able to earn higher salaries: the parent who provides less income typically becomes the primary care giver. Among high-income families, where either of the adults' salaries would provide sufficient support for the family, the decision becomes one of personal preference. At the same time, many stay-at-home-dads report being quizzed about their masculinity and their expected date of return to the workforce. They also cite difficulty being accepted by their female counterparts.

Equality movements are not only about altering the attitudes of individuals; they are also intended to change cultures.

Stay-at-home-dads Men who function as the primary caretaker of their child(ren) while their partner is the main earner. Also known as stay-at-home-fathers.

Glass ceiling The idea that there is an artificial limit to how high minority group members can ascend in political or large-scale corporate systems.

A   Stay-at-home-dad Qian Xiaofeng dries his daughter's hair in Shanghai, China, in 2017. He has learnt to design and make clothes for her.
B   Ellen Johnson Sirleaf, former president of Liberia, Joyce Banda, former president of Malawi, and Gwen K Young, director of the Global Women's Leadership Initiative and Women in Public Service Project at the Wilson Center, speak at the Concordia Summit in New York City in 2016.

B

Specifically, they seek to increase access to political, economic and cultural power. Allowing greater access to power does not inherently change masculinity's focus on power; it simply increases the number of competitors for that power. The past few decades have seen greater numbers of female candidates for local and national political offices, as well as powerful female heads of state such as Margaret Thatcher (1925–2013) and Angela Merkel (b. 1954). These changes have been more evident in Western nations than elsewhere, although some women in Asia – Chandrika Kumaratunga (b. 1945) in Sri Lanka, 1994–2005; Bidhya Devi Bhandari (b. 1961) in Nepal, 2015–present – and Africa – Luísa Diogo (b. 1958) in Mozambique, 2004–10; Joyce Banda (b. 1950) in Malawi, 2012–14 – have also attained these posts.

The idea that we should 'speak truth to power' relies on the assumption that power will recognize the statement as truth, feel empathy and then act accordingly. This is important because the glass ceiling is maintained by those who are above it, not by those it prevents from advancing. Thus, it must be destroyed by those who have something to lose: the men currently in charge.

A

Our notions of masculinity are also being challenged and shaped by our increasing awareness of people who are queer or transgender or intersex, and the idea that gender is fluid. Discussions of how to blend (stereotypical) masculine and feminine traits, beliefs and activities are not new, having been debated in the 1970s under the banner of androgyny.

A substantial amount of social science research at the end of the 20th century explored connections between androgyny and well-being. Generally speaking, women who possessed relatively high levels of both masculine and feminine traits fared better than women who possessed either feminine or masculine traits, but not both. Among men, there was no difference between those who had relatively high levels of masculine traits and those who possessed both masculine and feminine traits. These findings tell us that women benefit from 'adding' masculine traits to their behavioural repertoire while men do not 'lose' anything by adding feminine traits. Within this framework, the data indicate that masculinity is associated with good outcomes, such as higher self-esteem, greater sense of confidence and overall better mental health.

There are several challenges to blending gender roles in this way. One of the most obvious is that masculinity has an anti-femininity directive to which a man who chooses to blend masculine and feminine must diminish his adherence. There is not a comparable anti-masculinity directive within femininity.

Intersex Individuals born with variations in sex characteristics that do not fit the standard definitions for male or female bodies. Possible variations include chromosomes, gonads, sex hormones and genitals.

Androgyny Possessing, demonstrating or participating in both masculine and feminine characteristics, attributes and activities.

B

How do we think about – and try to address – questions about masculinity's future?

Feminists and pro-feminists use the assumptions, methods and principles developed for the study of women and femininity to explore issues related to men and masculinity, including the ideas that masculinity is socially constructed and that not all individuals enact masculinity in the same way. Many people adopt the pro-feminist label because they support principles of equality that are fundamental to feminist thought while not necessarily considering themselves part of the feminist movement.

By electing to use the term 'pro-feminist', men are crediting the feminist movement with founding the modern study of gender. However, there has been and continues to be substantial debate about whether or not men can truly be feminist. Can men really understand or devote themselves to feminism if they have never experienced its harmful effects?

A President of Chile Michelle Bachelet gives a speech during the presentation of the 'He for She' campaign on 12 April 2016 in Santiago, Chile. He for She is a global movement, sponsored by UN Women, for the creation of a gender equal world.

B UN Women global goodwill ambassador Emma Watson hugs Justin Trudeau, prime minister of Canada, at the He For She reception at the Museum of Modern Art, New York, on 20 September 2016.

C Hundreds of South Korean men, holding signs that read 'Opposition to Presumed Guilty', protest at a rally in Seoul in 2018 against the presumption of guilt often seen in #MeToo reports. A rally in support of female victims took place simultaneously in another part of the city.

c

These questions have resurfaced recently as part of #MeToo. The movement attempts to decrease rates of sexual assault and rape, as well as other aspects of rape culture, by increasing awareness and empathy on social media. It relies on survivors telling their stories of being victimized and thus encouraging men to act, in the future, according to their feelings for victims they know. As an Internet-based movement, #MeToo has been ambivalent towards male survivors of sexual assault and rape, with some women welcoming and encouraging men to share their stories of victimhood, and others positioning it as a women-only movement and encouraging men to use their own hashtags, such as #MenToo and #HeToo.

Pro-feminist Someone who supports feminism and gender equality, and who applies feminist research methods and assumptions to the understanding of men. Most often used in reference to male feminists.

#MeToo A movement to increase awareness of sexual assault that became well known on social media in 2017 in connection with and in response to the allegations against Harvey Weinstein. In 2018, questions about 'ownership' of the movement appeared to sap some of its energy and momentum.

A

A   Newly elected Canadian Prime Minister Justin Trudeau (fifth from left, front row) takes a group photograph with his gender and ethnically diverse cabinet ministers at Rideau Hall, Ottawa, Canada, in 2015.

B   Stills from Gillette's controversial 2019 advert for razors, in which the company's 30-year-old tag line 'The best a man can get' is replaced with 'The best men can be'. It attracted lavish praise and angry criticism in equal measure.

Many men's studies scholars identify as pro-feminist and view their work as complementing women's studies. They dominate the academic organizations devoted to the topic: the American Men's Studies Association and the Society for the Psychological Study of Men and Masculinities (a division of the American Psychological Association). A subsection of the British Psychological Association is focused on men and masculinity. To date, these groups have prioritized academic research but have relatively low public profiles.

Some pro-feminists are working to reduce men's violence against women by discussing alternatives to the manbox with groups of men. Examples include Tony Porter and his A Call to Men and Jackson Katz's MVP Programme.

Politicians such as Justin Trudeau (b. 1971), Emmanuel Macron (b. 1977) and Barack Obama (b. 1961) present an image of masculinity that highlights cooperation and collaboration, including the sharing of power. Canadian Prime Minister Trudeau, for example, explicitly created a cabinet that was demographically similar to the Canadian populace, rather than a cabinet that represented his own demographic groups. In 2017, French President Macron made gender equality his 'great cause'. These leaders' behaviour suggests they might identify as pro-feminist.

Some large corporations have also joined the conversation. For example, Nike's adverts in 2018 featuring American football player Colin Kaepernick encouraged people to 'Believe in something. Even if it means sacrificing everything.' In 2019, Gillette's razor commercial challenged men to be the best they can be in light of #MeToo.

A Call to Men A US-based organization devoted to creating a 'healthy, respectful manhood', with particular attention paid to reducing violence perpetrated by men.

MVP Programme The Mentors in Violence Prevention programme uses a bystander intervention approach to reduce sexual violence and bullying perpetrated by men.

Mythopoetic An approach to understanding men that draws from and focuses on symbolic expressions of masculinity found in myths, literature and religious ideals.

Some researchers and thinkers adopt a mythopoetic framework that focuses on archetypes. This approach was popularized by Robert Bly (b. 1926) in *Iron John: A Book about Men* (1990), which urged men to rediscover their core masculinity by gathering with other men in a rural setting and establishing a spiritual and emotional companionship. The Mankind Project, which has similar theoretical roots, currently has more than 1,000 peer-facilitated groups in 21 nations, including most of Europe and all of the English-speaking world. The Mankind Project's goals include bringing men together in peer-led, male-only settings that facilitate greater emotional intimacy and better quality male-male friendships, and thus produce happier and better adjusted men.

B

Academic programmes in women's studies, sexuality studies and ethnic minority studies have helped expand our knowledge and understanding of the experiences of these groups at both individual and cultural levels. They have fostered activism that has contributed to increased legal equality and social changes over the past few decades. This suggests that universities should teach more courses focused on masculinity or have men's studies programmes.

If we truly want to understand masculinity, including its origins and how to change it, then formal study of it would seem to be in order. In the academic year 2018/19, there appears to be only one bachelor's level (Hobart and William Smith Colleges, USA) and one master's level (Stony Brook, USA) programme focused specifically on men, although institutions such as the University of Calgary, Leeds Beckett University and Queensland University of Technology all have faculties that conduct research on men and masculinities.

A

Good Men Project
A magazine-style website geared towards discussing issues that men face today, primarily from a pro-feminist perspective.

B

A   Students on the first women's studies course at Queen's University, Kingston, Canada, in 1985. Such courses are common today, but men's studies courses are rare.
B   Undergraduate Kevin Okifo leads a discussion about toxic masculinity on the University of Connecticut campus in 2019.
C   A participant in the San Francisco Women's March in 2019 challenges men to reject toxic masculinity.

c

The discussion about how to change masculinity is not limited to academics and activists; it is a conversation in which anyone can participate.

Online, the Good Men Project advertises that it is hosting 'the conversation no one else is having'. Its name points to an important question: What does it mean to be a good man? Given what we now know about the West's dominant conception of masculinity, it seems clear that a good man will necessarily adhere to a different definition of masculinity.

Conclusion

A Pub life and drinking beer are an intrinsic part of Czech culture, and contribute to the Czech Republic's first place world ranking in annual consumption of beer per capita, at 156 litres (34 gal). Is a beer belly worth the benefit of cultural inclusion?

B Tattoos are often used to indicate gang membership as well as simply to express individuality. Texas prison officials use prisoners' tattoos to determine where they will be placed, including for solitary confinement.

So, is masculinity toxic? It is complicated, and the answer is both 'Yes' – the current dominant cultural masculine ideal we have labelled the manbox is clearly harmful – and 'No' – most men are not toxic because they do not adhere strongly enough to these dictates to cause harm. Different harms are exhibited by different groups, and even by different individuals within a single group.

Western notions of masculinity are geared towards teaching men to have and wield power, and these ideals work in coordination with other cultural systems to restrict who has access to that power. Thus, sexism, racism, heterosexism and social class all intersect with masculinity to facilitate men's power and a patriarchal culture. But even among men who fit all the right demographic categories, there is still competition for power and its benefits, and not all men choose to compete. Those who fail at this competition are marginalized and may be harmed, and even killed, in the process of competing for masculinity's benefits.

More specifically, the current dominant version of masculinity readily lends itself to various harms by allowing violence and a broad spectrum of risk-taking, encouraging men to prioritize their earnings over their health, inhibiting men from attending to a wide range of feelings, including empathy, and discouraging them from forming intimate relationships. This contributes to men having shorter lifespans than women, to men's violence against women and to decisions by the dominant groups of men to limit access to power by women and other men. It also contributes to men being less emotionally intimate with others and having fewer high-quality relationships, at least in comparison to women.

B

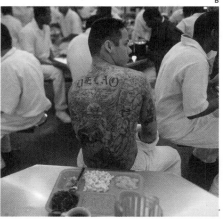

For individual men, toxicity appears primarily among those who have high levels of adherence to hegemonic masculinity. A rigid adherence to the manbox's definition without allowing flexibility is problematic: it prevents these men from adapting to individual situations and cultural changes.

At the same time, not all aspects of masculinity are bad. Around the world, men want to be seen as honourable, to be in control of their own lives and to have a good job, and they are not particularly interested in being promiscuous. Risking one's body or life in order to defend or care for others, as first responders and members of the military do, is also rooted in some of these same directives. Scientific research and capitalism both reward risk-taking, albeit in different ways that may or may not be beneficial. Being a financial provider, even the primary breadwinner, is not inherently bad. Having a clearer understanding of masculinity's positive aspects could provide a roadmap for increasing masculinity's benefits while simultaneously working to limit its toxicity. Such a rebalancing of masculinity would facilitate an easier transition for men who have been raised in the current system, while minimizing objections from those who fear radical change.

A

B

A   Men stretch during a yoga class in Sydney, Australia. Men's increasing participation in yoga counters the macho image of Australian men and suggests that a rebalancing of competitiveness and calming may be in progress.

B   Journalist Marie Colvin (second from left) poses for a photograph with Libyan rebels in Misrata in 2011. She died while covering the siege of Homs in Syria in 2012.

Most men today report low to moderate levels of adherence to hegemonic masculinity, especially when its individual aspects present as problematic behaviour or rigidity to masculine norms. In fact, it appears that #NotAllMen conforms to the English-speaking world's definition of masculinity; there is only room for one alpha male in any group, and only a few in society in general. If most men are not particularly masculine, what does that mean for masculinity?

Perhaps we need to stop assuming that hegemonic masculinity is relevant to all men and start talking about the manbox ideals as designed primarily to facilitate men's leadership in social groups and society as a whole. If that is what masculinity is about, maybe we would be better served by labelling it as such and recognizing that only a minority of individuals – male or female – want to be leaders and prefer an aggressive style of leadership. This approach would provide space for most men to conform to a set of 'everyman' standards, potentially centred around notions of what it means to be a good man.

A

What kind of men do we want? What can we do to ameliorate aspects of masculinity that are toxic? What traits would we like to see as making up a new masculine ideal?

Perhaps we need to be more explicit in creating and encouraging multiple masculinities, and ridding ourselves of the idea that there is only one true masculine ideal with all other forms ranked below it. We could imagine each type of masculinity as a collection of desirable component qualities, behaviours and roles. Every man could select a set of qualities to create his own personal masculinity. No one set needs to be considered any better than any other, thus abolishing a hierarchy of masculinities.

A   Discussion of who men are and who men should be continues. Rose Cameron, of Leo Burnett advertising agency, identified four types of masculine profile that might be marketed to. They are, from left to right: retrosexual, patriarch, metrosexual and power seeker. Each type evokes different aspects and conceptions of masculinity. Should any one type be the primary, hegemonic form of masculinity by which all versions of masculinity are judged? Or should we accept that multiple forms of masculinity are equally valid, each composed of a collection of qualities, and each able to coexist without the need for hierarchy?

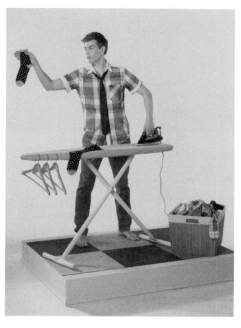

How could we put forward such an idea to maximize its reach? Part of the answer is to increase everyone's awareness and thinking about masculinity. We could all discuss its negative and positive aspects; the traits we like and dislike; the elements that underpin a patriarchal society. We should also discuss female masculinity (or being 'butch'), queer masculinity and trans men's masculinity. Finally, we might also give more thought to our choices. When we click, purchase or vote, we provide some level of credence and support for a particular version of masculinity.

Whatever your thoughts, it is clear that change is upon us. These changes affect everyone, of all genders, and we must all have a voice in determining what our cultural standards of masculinity will be.

Further Reading

Addis, M. E., *Invisible Men: Men's Inner Lives and the Consequences of Silence* (New York, NY: Times Books, 2011)

Addis, M. E. and Mahalik, J. R., 'Men, Masculinity, and the Contexts of Help Seeking', *American Psychologist*, 2003, 58, 5–14

Archer, J., 'Testosterone and Human Aggression: An Evaluation of the Challenge Hypothesis', *Neuroscience and Biobehavioral Reviews*, 2006, 30 (3), 319–45

Bly, R., *Iron John* (Reading, MA: Addison-Wesley, 1990)

Carroll, H., *Affirmative Reaction: New Formations of White Masculinity* (Durham, NC: Duke University Press, 2011)

Coad, D., *The Metrosexual: Gender, Sexuality, and Sport* (Albany, NY: State University of New York Press, 2008)

Connell, R. W., *Masculinities* (Berkeley, CA: University of California Press, 1995)

Coontz, S., *The Way We Never Were*, 2nd ed. (New York, NY: Basic Books, 2016)

Cooper, A. and Smith, E. L., *Homicide Trends in the United States, 1980–2008* (Washington, DC: Bureau of Justice Statistics, 2011)

Courtenay, W. H., *Dying to Be Men: Psychosocial, Environmental, and Biobehavioral Directions in Promoting the Health of Men and Boys* (New York, NY: Routledge, 2011)

Crosby, A. E., Ortega, L. and Stevens, M. R., 'Suicides – United States, 2005–2009', *Mortality and Morbidity Weekly Review*, 2013, 62, 179–83

David, D. and Brannon, R., 'The Male Sex Role: Our Culture's Blueprint for Manhood and What It's Done for Us Lately' in D. David and R. Brannon (eds.), *The Forty-nine Percent Majority: The Male Sex Role* (Reading, MA: Addison-Wesley, 1976) 1–48

Farrell, W., *The Myth of Male Power* (New York, NY: Berkley Books, 1993)

Garfield, R., *Breaking the Male Code: Unlocking the Power of Friendship* (New York, NY: Gotham, 2013)

Heilman, B., Levtov, R., van der Gaag, N., Hassink, A. and Barker, G., *State of the World's Fathers: Time for Action* (Washington, DC: Promundo, Sonke Gender Justice, Save the Children, and MenEngage Alliance, 2017)

Hodapp, C., *Men's Rights, Gender, and Social Media* (Lanham, MD: Lexington Books, 2017)

Huntington, Samuel P., *The Third Wave: Democratization in the Late Twentieth Century* (Norman: University of Oklahoma Press, 1991)

Kilmartin, C. and Allison, J., *Men's Violence Against Women: Theory, Research, and Activism* (Mahwah, NJ: Erlbaum, 2007)

Kimmel, M., *Manhood in America: A Cultural History* (New York, NY: The Free Press, 1996)

Kuo, P. X. and Ward, L. M., 'Contributions of Television Use to Beliefs About Fathers and Gendered Family Roles Among First-Time Expectant Parents', *Psychology of Men and Masculinity*, 17, 352–362

Lamb, M. E., 'Mothers, Fathers, Families, and Circumstances: Factors Affecting Children's Adjustment', *Applied Developmental Science*, 2012, 16 (2), 98–111

Levant, R. F. and Wong, Y. J., *The Psychology of Men and Masculinities* (Washington, DC: American Psychological Association, 2017)

Livingston, G., *Growing Number of Dads Home with the Kids: Biggest Increase Among Those Caring for Family* (Washington, DC: Pew Research Centre, 2014)

Lynch, J. R. and Kilmartin, C., *Overcoming Masculine Depression: The Pain Behind the Mask*, 2nd ed. (New York, NY: Routledge/Taylor & Francis Group, 2013)

Ng, C. J., Tan, H. M. and Low, W. Y., 'What do Asian men consider as important masculinity attributes? Findings from the Asian Men's Attitudes to Life Events and Sexuality (MALES) Study' *Journal of Men's Health*, 2008, 5 (4), 350–55

O'Neil, J. M., *Men's Gender Role Conflict: Psychological Costs, Consequences, and an Agenda for Change* (Washington, DC: American Psychological Association, 2015)

Pascoe, C. J., *Dude, You're a Fag: Masculinity and Sexuality in High School* (Berkeley, CA: University of California Press, 2007)

Pleck, J. H., 'Why Could Father Involvement Benefit Children? Theoretical perspectives', *Applied Developmental Science*, 2007, 11 (4), 196–202

Pope, H. G., Phillips, K. A. and Olivardia, R., *The Adonis Complex: The Secret Crisis of Male Body Obsessions* (New York, NY: The Free Press, 2000)

Rotundo, E. A., *American Manhood: Transformations in Masculinity from the Revolution to the Modern Era* (New York, NY: Basic Books, 1993)

Smiler, A. P., *Challenging Casanova: Beyond the Steroetype of Promiscuous Young Male Sexuality* (San Francisco: Jossey-Bass, 2013)

Smiler, A. P. and Kilmartin, C., *The Masculine Self*, 6th ed. (Cornwall on Hudson, NY: Sloan Publishing, 2019)

Stearns, P. N., *American Cool: Constructing a Twentieth-Century Emotional Style* (New York, NY: New York University Press, 1994)

Townsend, K., *Manhood at Harvard: William James and others* (Cambridge, MA: Harvard University Press, 1996)

Twenge, J. M., *Generation Me: Why Today's Young Americans are More Confident, Assertive, Entitled – and More Miserable Than Ever Before* (New York, NY: Free Press, 2006)

Way, N. and Chu, J. Y., *Adolescent Boys: Exploring Diverse Cultures of Boyhood* (New York, NY: New York University Press, 2004)

Way, N., *Deep Secrets: Boys' Friendships and the Crisis of Connection* (Cambridge, MA: Harvard University Press, 2011)

Wong, Y. J. and Wester, S. R., *American Psychological Association Handbook of Men and Masculinities* (Washington, DC: American Psychological Association, 2016)

Picture Credits

Every effort has been made to locate and credit copyright holders of the material reproduced in this book. The author and publisher apologise for any omissions or errors, which can be corrected in future editions.

a = above, b = below,
c = centre, l = left, r = right

Clinical and pathologic findings, by A.L. Jones, J.W. Britton, M.M. Blessing, J.E. Parisi, G.D. Cascino, 2018. ncbi.nlm.nih.gov/ pubmed/29321231

64 Clive Mason / Getty Images

65 Alberto Simon / AFP / Getty Images

66 Hero Images / Getty Images

67 a Vova Pomortzeff / Alamy Stock Photo

67 b BSIP/UIG / Getty Images

68 Perry van Munster / Alamy Stock Photo

69 Dan Kitwood / Getty Images

70 Ron Sachs – Pool / Getty Images

71 Artwork by Sarah Gochrach for *Equal Means Equal*

72 a Robyn Beck / AFP / Getty Images

72 b David McNew / Getty Images

73 ohanabira.wordpress. com/2012/07/28/otaku- als-trendwort/169308_43 43893844254_155843660 1_o/ and blog.livedoor.jp/ itabeya

74 Courtesy Angela Washko

75 NurPhoto.com / Alamy Stock Photo

76 Peter Kovalev / TASS / Getty Images

78 David Coleman / Alamy Stock Photo

79 a Luis Sinco / Los Angeles Times / Getty Images

79 b Sandy Huffaker / Getty Images

80 Cristina Quicler / AFP / Getty Images

81 Agencja Fotograficzna Caro / Alamy Stock Photo

82–3 Courtesy the artist Nicolai Howalt and Martin Asbæk Gallery, Copenhagen

84 Robert Fried / Alamy Stock Photo

85 Dan Kitwood / Getty Images

86 l Sleep Pretty in Pink, www.hearos.com

86 r Skull Screw Ear Plugs, www.hearos.com

87 l Freshbakedva.com

87 c Sweetbyholly.com

87 r Twitter

88 a domonabikeSpain / Alamy Stock Photo

88 b Jed Leicester / Getty Images

89 Arisha Singh / Alamy Stock Photo

90 Satoshi Takahashi / LightRocket / Getty Images

91 l Pep Roig / Alamy Stock Photo

91 r Franck Metois / Alamy Stock Photo

92 Giulia Marchi / The Washington Post / Getty Images

93 UK Says No More

94 Nordicphotos / Alamy Stock Photo

95 a Matthew Horwood / Alamy Stock Photo

95 b Brendan Bell / Alamy Stock Photo

96 Frederic J. Brown / AFP / Getty Images

97 Andrew Burton / Getty Images

98 Jd / Keystone USA / Shutterstock

99 *Neural Correlates of Sexual Cue Reactivity in Individuals with and without Compulsive Sexual Behaviours*, by V. Voon, T.B. Mole, P. Banca, L. Porter, L. Morris, S. Mitchell, et al, 2014. PLoS ONE 9(7): e102419. doi.org/10.1371/ journal.pone.0102419

100 Satsuma Designs

101 Matt Alexander / PA Archive / PA Images

102 ThinkProgress

103 a Reuters / Eva Plevier

103 b Reuters / Kim Hong-Ji

104–5 Shi Yangkun / VCG / Getty Images

106 Kyodo News / Getty Images

107 Spencer Platt / Getty Images

108 Carolyn Drake / Magnum Photos

109 Constantine Manos / Magnum Photos

110 Reuters / Chip East CME

111 a John Moore / Getty Images

111 b Peter van Agtmael / Magnum Photos

112 Courtesy Movember Foundation

113 Matt Rourke / AP / Shutterstock

114 Rob Walls / Alamy Stock Photo

115 a Halfpoint / Shutterstock

115 b DisobeyArt / Shutterstock

116 Promundo

117 a Andrew Spear / The Washington Post / Getty Images

117 b Georges Gobet / AFP / Getty Images

118 Shi Yangkun / VCG / Getty Images

119 Paul Morigi / Getty Images for Concordia Summit

120 Mustafa Yalcin / Anadolu Agency / Getty Images

121 Jewel Samad / AFP / Getty Images

122 a Sebastian Vivallo Onate / Agencia Makro / LatinContent / Getty Images

122 b Rob Kim / Getty Images

123 Jean Chung / Getty Images

124 Xinhua / Alamy Stock Photo

125 Gillette

126 a Queen's University, Kingston, Canada

126 b Hanaisha Lewis

127 Sundry Photography / Shutterstock.com

128–9 Tim Clayton / Corbis / Getty Images

130 Sean Gallup / Getty Images

131 a Reuters / Ulises Rodriguez

131 b Andrew Lichtenstein / Getty Images

132 Greg Wood / AFP / Getty Images

133 Reuters / Zohra Bensemra

134–5 Saverio Truglia / Chicago Tribune / MCT / Getty Images

Index

Acknowledgments:
I would like to thank my wife and daughter
for their support while I worked on this project.
Your love helps sustain me.

My thanks also to the team at Thames
& Hudson: Jane Laing, Tristan de Lancey,
Phoebe Lindsley and Isabel Jessop.

First published in the United Kingdom in 2019
by Thames & Hudson Ltd, 181A High Holborn,
London WC1V 7QX

General Editor: Matthew Taylor

British Library Cataloguing-in-Publication Data
A catalogue record for this book is available from
the British Library

ISBN 978-0-500-29502-1

Printed and bound in Slovenia by
DZS-Grafik d.o.o

To find out about all our publications,
please visit **www.thamesandhudson.com**.
There you can subscribe to our e-newsletter,
browse or download our current catalogue,
and buy any titles that are in print.